Keep Cool!

Englisch zur Berufsvorbereitung

Andrew K. Johnson

Ernst Klett Schulbuchverlage
Stuttgart · Leipzig

Keep Cool!

Englisch zur Berufsvorbereitung

von

Andrew K. Johnson, Cambridge

Gaby Fruhmann, Hörmannsdorf (Activity pages)

Beratung

Ursula Jäger, Pforzheim

Werksübersicht

Lehr- / Arbeitsbuch 3-12-808103-4

Lehrerhandbuch mit Lehrer-Audio-CD 3-12-808106-9

1. Auflage 1 5 4 3 2 1 | 2010 2009 2008 2007 2006

Alle Drucke dieser Auflage sind unverändert (und können im Unterricht nebeneinander verwendet werden). Die letzte Zahl bezeichnet das Jahr des Druckes.

Internetadresse: www.klett.de

Redaktion: Helen Smyth
Gestaltung und Umschlag: B2 Gestaltung, Andreas Staiger, Stuttgart
Grafiken: Katrin Wolff, Wiesbaden
Reproduktion: Meyle + Müller, Medien-Management, Pforzheim
Druck: Wachter GmbH, Bönnigheim

Printed in Germany.
ISBN-13: 978-3-12-808103-8
ISBN-10: 3-12-808103-4

9 783128 081038

Inhaltsverzeichnis

Vorwort

Keep Cool! richtet sich an Schülerinnen und Schüler im Berufsvorbereitungsjahr sowie an Lernende in berufsvorbereitenden Kursen mit niedrigem Einstiegsniveau, die wenige oder keine Vorkenntnisse im Fach Englisch haben.

Die Lehrwerksteile umfassen:
- Das einbändige Lehr-/Arbeitsbuch zum Reinschreiben.
- Das Lehrerhandbuch mit einer Lehrer-Audio-CD. Das Handbuch enthält Lösungen, methodische Hinweise, Vorschläge für einen handlungsorientierten Unterricht, landeskundliche Informationen, eine Übersicht über die wichtigsten Lernziele der einzelnen Units sowie Kopiervorlagen mit zusätzlichem Übungsmaterial.

Zielsetzung
Keep Cool! vermittelt Lernenden mit einem niedrigem bis sehr niedrigem Einstiegsniveau folgende Kompetenzen:
- Anwendung elementarer Kommunikationsmittel zu altersrelevanten Themen in der Weltsprache Englisch,
- Erfassen der Kernaussagen von gesprochenem und geschriebenem Englisch,
- Textproduktion mit starker Lenkung durch die Lehrkraft,
- Zusammenarbeit mit einem Partner oder in der Gruppe,
- Selbstevaluation,
- Verständnis einer Basisgrammatik Englisch.

Aufbau des Lehr-/Arbeitsbuches
Die sieben klar strukturierten Units sind thematisch aufgebaut und enthalten folgende Schwerpunkte:
- **Lead-in** Einführung in die Thematik der Unit.
- **Speaking** Bereitstellung und Anwendung (besonders in Partnerarbeit) von Redemitteln.
- **Listening** Hörverstehenstexte (HV) mit Übungen. Die HV-Texte befinden sich auf der Lehrer-Audio-CD ◎. Die einzelnen Trackpunkte sind neben der jeweiligen Aufgabe notiert (T1).
- **Reading** Lesetexte mit Übungen zum Leseverstehen. Diese Texte sind ebenfalls auf der Lehrer-Audio-CD ◎ und im Lehr-/ Arbeitsbuch mit dem jeweiligen Trackpunkt versehen.
- **Writing** Übungen zu den eingeführten Redemitteln, zum Wortschatz und zur Grammatik.
- **Checking** Überprüfung des Gelernten, Selbsteinschätzung und eine Übersicht der wichtigsten Grammatikthemen in der Unit.

Im Anhang finden Sie:
- eine Liste der wichtigsten unregelmäßigen Verben,
- eine kapitelbegleitende Wortliste (englisch-deutsch),
- eine alphabetische Wortliste (deutsch-englisch),
- alle Hörverstehenstexte.

Auf vier Sonderseiten finden Sie **Activity pages**, die zum Ausschneiden und Einsatz in Partner- und Gruppenarbeit geeignet sind.

Viel Spaß und Erfolg bei der Arbeit mit diesem Buch wünschen Ihnen

Autor, Beraterin und Redaktion

About me 1

1 Anne and Pete

I am Pete.
I am English.
I am seventeen.
I am cool.

I am Anne.
I'm from England.
I'm sixteen.
I'm cool, too.

A Finish the sentences.
Vervollständigen Sie die Sätze.

1. The boy in the photo is Pete.
2. He is from England ______.
3. He's ______.
4. ______ cool.
5. The girl ______ is Anne.
6. She is ______.
7. She's ______.
8. ______ cool, too.

B And you? Write about yourself.
Schreiben Sie über sich.

1. I'm ______.
2. I'm from ______.
3. I'm ______.
4. ______ cool.

C What's cool, Anne and Pete?

1. England is cool.
2. MTV ______ cool.
3. Music ______ cool.
4. CDs are cool.
5. MP3 players are ______.
6. Discos ______.

D And you? What's cool? Write six sentences.
Schreiben Sie sechs Sätze in Ihr Heft.

2 Brothers and sisters

Here are Sue and Jill.
They are my sisters.
Sue is eleven.
Jill is fourteen.

Here are Tom and John.
They're my brothers.
Tom is thirteen.
John is eighteen.

Sue 11

Jill 14

Tom 13

John 18

A Finish the sentences.

Vervollständigen Sie die Sätze.

Andy 16

Sarah 13

Julia 18

Sharon 16

Ben 11

Mark 14

1. Here are Sarah and Julia.
2. They're my ____________.
3. Sarah is ____________.
4. Julia is ____________.
5. Here are ____________.
6. They're ____________.
7. Ben ____________.
8. Mark ____________.

B Read the dialogue.

Lesen Sie den Dialog.

Tim: Hi. You are Paula.
Mary: I'm not Paula. I'm Mary. Are you Tim?
Tim: Yes, I am.

C Now you. Act dialogues with a partner.

Partnerarbeit. Führen Sie Dialoge zu zweit.

3 Families

A **Listen to the CD. Match the texts (1, 2, 3, 4) with the photos.**
Hören Sie die CD an. Welcher Text (1, 2, 3, 4) passt zu welchem Foto?

B **Look at the photos in A and finish the sentences.**
Schauen Sie die Fotos in A an und vervollständigen Sie die Sätze.

Paula: 1. I have got two brothers.
Joe: 2. I haven't got ________.
3. I've got ________.
Leo: 4. ________ a brother.
5. I ________ a sister.
Maggie: 6. ________ two sisters.
7. I ________ a brother.

C **And you? Write about your brothers and sisters.**
Schreiben Sie etwas über Ihre Geschwister in Ihr Heft.

D **Listen to the CD. What does Dot say?**
Hören Sie die CD an. Was sagt Dot?

1. I've got a book.
2. ________ a CD.
3. ________ a partner.
4. ________ a sister.

E **Write about Dot.**
Schreiben Sie über Dot.

Example: **Dot has got a book. She hasn't got …**

4 An email from England

T3 **A Read this email.**
Lesen Sie diese E-Mail.

From: Rachel Lee <rachel@keepcool.us>
To: Daniel Fischer <danielf@keepcool.us>
Date: 04-03

Hi,

I'm Rachel Lee. I'm at college in Bristol. Bristol is in England. I've got cool teachers. They're very friendly. My favourite teacher is Mr Baker. He's my German teacher. Are you at college too? Have you got a job?

I've got a brother, Robert. He is twelve. No, he's thirteen now. Robert and I are football fans. We are Manchester United fans. What's your favourite football team? Is it Bayern Munich?

I haven't got a sister, but that's OK. My mother and father are fun. They're cool parents. And I've got lots of good friends. And now you're one of my friends too!

Best wishes,
Rachel

PS There are photos with this email. There's a good photo of me and my brother with Toby, our cat.

B True or false? Put a ✗ in the correct box.
Richtig oder falsch? Kreuzen Sie an.

	True	False
1. Rachel is at college in Bristol.	☒	☐
2. Rachel's favourite teacher is Mrs Baxter.	☐	☐
3. Rachel has got a brother.	☐	☐
4. She has got a sister.	☐	☐
5. Her favourite football team is Bayern Munich.	☐	☐
6. She has got lots of good friends.	☐	☐

5 Practice page

A Finish this email about yourself to Rachel.
Vervollständigen Sie diese E-Mail an Rachel. Schreiben Sie über sich.
Tipp: Die E-Mail von Rachel auf Seite 8 hilft Ihnen dabei.

I'm ______________. I'm at ______________ in ______________.
______________ is in Germany. My favourite teacher is ______________.
______________ got a cat. My ______________ football team
is ______________.
Best wishes, ______________

B Write the missing numbers in words.
Schreiben Sie die fehlenden Zahlen in Wörtern.

1	one	11	______	22	twenty-two
2	______	12	twelve	30	thirty
3	three	13	______	33	thirty-______
4	four	14	______	44	forty-______
5	five	15	fifteen	55	fifty-______
6	six	16	______teen	66	sixty-______
7	seven	17	______teen	77	seventy-______
8	______	18	______teen	88	eighty-______
9	nine	19	______teen	99	ninety-______
10	ten	20	twenty	101	a hundred and ______

C Write the short forms.
Schreiben Sie die Kurzformen.

1. I am ______________
2. You are ______________
3. He is ______________
4. We are ______________
5. I have got ______________
6. We have got ______________

D Write the questions.
Schreiben Sie die Fragen.

1. You're English. Are you English?
2. He's a fan. Is ______________?
3. They're brothers. Are ______________?
4. You've got a sister. Have ______________?

6 Check your English

A Fill in the missing words.
Ergänzen Sie die fehlenden Wörter.

1. Hi. I 'm ______________________ (Ihr Name).
2. I ______________ at college in Germany.
3. Pat ______________ got two brothers.
4. But she hasn't ______________ a sister.
5. Are ______________ a Bayern Munich fan? – No!!!
6. My brothers ______________ cool, very cool!
7. Jürgen: I'm German. I ______________ English.
8. ____________________ a brother? – No, but I've got a sister.
9. 112 is a hundred and ______________.

B Draw the correct number of icons in the circles.
Malen Sie die richtige Anzahl an Smilies in die Kreise.

☺☺☺ Kann ich schon! ☺☺ Kann ich ein bisschen! ☺ Kann ich bald!

1. Ich kann sagen, wie ich heiße. ○○○
2. Ich kann über Geschwister sprechen. ○○○
3. Ich kann eine Aussage machen. ○○○
4. Ich kann einen Satz verneinen. ○○○
5. Ich kann Fragen stellen. ○○○
6. Ich kann auf Englisch zählen. ○○○

Present tense Gegenwart

► **to be**

Positive Aussage	Verneinung	Frage
I'm (I am)	I'm not (I am not)	Am I?
You're (You are)	You aren't (You are not)	Are you?
He's / She's / It's (He / She / It is)	He / She / It isn't (He / She / It is not)	Is he / she / it?
We're (We are)	We aren't (We are not)	Are we?
You're (You are)	You aren't (You are not)	Are you?
They're (They are)	They aren't (They are not)	Are they?

► **has / have got**

Positive Aussage	Verneinung	Frage
I've got (I have got)	I haven't got (I have not got)	Have I got?
You've got (You have got)	You haven't got (You have not got)	Have you got?
He / She / It's got (He / She / It has got)	He / She / It hasn't got (He / She / It has not got)	Has he / she / it got?
We've got (We have got)	We haven't got (We have not got)	Have we got?
You've got (You have got)	You haven't got (You have not got)	Have you got?
They've got (They have got)	They haven't got (They have not got)	Have they got?

Free time 2

1 Teenagers and free time

A Match the verbs and words in the boxes to the photos.
Ordnen Sie die Verben und Wörter in den Kästen den Fotos zu.

drive sit watch ~~go~~ go
~~play~~ get up visit meet

to the disco a car at 6 o'clock friends TV
at the computer ~~to the cinema~~ ~~sport~~ family

In the week

1. Teenagers play sport.

2. They ______

3. ______

4. ______

5. ______

6. ______

At the weekend

7. Teenagers often go to the cinema.

8. They sometimes ______

9. They never ______ on Saturdays.

B And your free time? Write sentences in your exercise book.
Was machen Sie in Ihrer Freizeit? Schreiben Sie Sätze in Ihr Heft.

Example: I sometimes go to the cinema.

2 Email friends

A Look at the photos and read the texts. Who's a good email friend for you?
Schauen Sie die Fotos an und lesen Sie die Texte. Wer kommt als E-Mail-Freund(in) für Sie in Frage?

Sandra Jones, 17
"I like shopping, cats and dogs, TV soaps, walking and pop music."

Pete Lee, 18
"I like motorbikes, discos, football, rap music and computer games."

Sue Potts, 18
"I like pop music discos, magazines, TV soaps and shopping."

Tony Day, 17
"I like walking, books, cars, cats and tennis."

I think ____________ is a good email friend for me because

I like ______________________________________, too.

B Talk about your email friend.
Sagen Sie, was Ihr E-Mail-Freund oder Ihre E-Mail-Freundin mag.

Example: **Tony likes walking, books and cars.**

C Anna's morning. Look at the pictures and complete the sentences.
Schauen Sie die Bilder an und vervollständigen Sie die Sätze.

07:00 get up

07:30 have breakfast

08:15 leave

08:45 arrive at college

1. Anna gets up at **seven o'clock**.
2. She has breakfast at ______________________.
3. She leaves ______________________.
4. She arrives at college ______________________.

= half past one

= quarter past one

= quarter to two

D And your morning? Tell a partner.
Partnerarbeit. Sagen Sie, was Sie morgens machen.

Example: **I get up at seven o'clock.**

3 Anna's Saturday

A Listen to the CD and number the pictures.
Hören Sie die CD an. Nummerieren Sie die Bilder in der Reihenfolge wie auf der CD.

B It's Saturday! Finish the sentences.
Es ist Samstag! Vervollständigen Sie die Sätze.

1. On Saturday Anna does not __go__ to college. She __goes__ to the shops.
2. She doesn't ____________ her friends at college. She ____________ them at MacBurger.
3. In the afternoon she doesn't ____________ in college. She ____________ at her computer.
4. In the evening she doesn't ____________ her friends. She ____________ her boyfriend.

C Write about your Saturday in your exercise book.
Schreiben Sie über Ihren Samstag in Ihr Heft.

Example: **I don't go to college. I play football.**

D Listen to the CD. Who is Anna's brother, Jim or Tim?
Hören Sie die CD an. Wer ist Annas Bruder, Jim oder Tim?

____

E Listen to the CD. Underline the correct verb form for Tim.
Hören Sie die CD an. Unterstreichen Sie die richtige Verbform für Tim.

1. I (<u>like</u>/do not like) music.
2. I (speak/don't speak) German.
3. I (like/don't like) magazines.
4. I (watch/don't watch) TV.
5. I (ride/don't ride) a motorbike.
6. I (play/don't play) football.

4 Free time in England

T6 **A** **Read the text below.**
Lesen Sie den unten stehenden Text.

Doctors say lots of teenagers aren't sporty. They sit in front of the TV, in the cinema or at the computer. They don't walk very often. In the week, from Monday to Friday, they go to college by bus or by car. They don't walk at the weekend. On Saturday and Sunday they watch TV, or they visit a friend and they watch more TV. But teenagers aren't stupid, doctors say. They know that sport is good for them. But they don't do it!

B **Fill in the missing words.**
Vervollständigen Sie die Sätze.

1. Doctors say lots of teenagers aren't sporty.
2. Doctors say they sit in front of the ______.
3. ____________ don't walk very often.
4. In the week they go to college by bus or by ______.
5. At the ____________ they watch TV or visit a friend.
6. Teenagers know that ________ is good for them.

C **Fill in the words from the box. The text can help you.**
Vervollständigen Sie die Sätze. Benutzen Sie die Wörter im Kasten. Der Text hilft Ihnen dabei.

1. There are lots of unsporty teenagers in England.
2. Tom often sits in front ______ the TV.
3. But he plays sport ______ college.
4. Lots of teenagers go ______ college ______ bus.
5. They don't walk ______ the weekend.
6. They know that sport is good ______ them.

of to at by
~~in~~ for at

D **Write about yourself. Choose the correct words.**
Schreiben Sie über sich. Suchen Sie die richtigen Wörter aus.

1. I (play/don't play) ________________ sport in my free time.
2. I (walk/don't walk) ________________ very often.
3. I (go/don't go) ________________ to college by car.
4. I (watch/don't watch) ________________ TV at the weekend.
5. I (think/don't think) ________________ sport is fun.

5 Practice page

A Complete the sentences.
Vervollständigen Sie die Sätze.

1. Bastian Schweinsteiger (lives/live) ___lives___ in Munich.
2. I (lives/live) __________ in __________.
3. Bastian Schweinsteiger (plays/play) __________ football.
4. I (plays/play) __________.
5. Bastian Schweinsteiger (speaks/speak) __________ German.
6. I (speak/speaks) __________.

B Complete the table with the days of the week.
Vervollständigen Sie die Tabelle mit den Wochentagen.

1.	Montag	Monday
2.	__________	Tuesday
3.	__________	Wednesday
4.	__________	Thursday
5.	Freitag	__________
6.	Samstag	__________
7.	Sonntag	__________

C What time is it? Write the time.
Wie spät ist es? Schreiben Sie die Uhrzeit auf.

1. 8.50: ___It's ten to nine___.

2. 8.55: It's __________ to nine.

3. 9.00: It's __________.

4. 9.05: It's __________.

5. 9.10: It's __________.

6. 9.15: It's __________.

6 Check your English

A **Write the sentences in English.**
Schreiben Sie die Sätze auf Englisch.

1. Ich gehe in die Disko. I go to the disco ______________.
2. Ich sehe oft fern. ______________.
3. Kevin treibt manchmal Sport. ______________.
4. Anna steht um acht Uhr auf. ______________.
5. Jane steht nie um sieben Uhr auf. ______________.
6. Es ist Freitag. ______________.
7. Teenager mögen Musik. ______________.
8. Paul mag keine Katzen. ______________.
9. Es ist Viertel nach neun. ______________.

B **Draw the correct number of icons in the circles.**
Malen Sie die richtige Anzahl an Smilies in die Kreise.

Kann ich schon! Kann ich ein bisschen! Kann ich bald!

1. Ich kann sagen, was jemand (oft) macht.
2. Ich kann sagen, was jemand nicht macht.
3. Ich kann sagen, was jemand mag.
4. Ich kann sagen, was jemand nicht mag.
5. Ich kann die Uhrzeit angeben.
6. Ich kann die Wochentage benennen.

Simple present Gegenwart

Positive Aussage	Verneinung
I play	I don't play (I do not play)
You play	You don't play (You do not play)
He / She / It plays	He / She / It doesn't play (He / She / It does not play)
We play	We don't play (We do not play)
You play	You don't play (You do not play)
They play	They don't play (They do not play)

Anwendung
Das **simple present** steht bei regelmäßigen oder wiederholten Handlungen und Gewohnheiten. Man findet häufig **sometimes** (manchmal), **often** (oft) und **never** (nie) beim **simple present**.

Examples: Tim sometimes rides his motorbike to college.
We often sit at the computer.
Anna and Paul never go shopping.

Image and style 3

1 Cool or not?

A **Which clothes are cool? Talk to a partner about the clothes in the photos.**
Partnerarbeit. Welche Kleidungstücke auf den Fotos finden Sie cool?

Example: **I (don't) think the clothes in photo 1 are cool.**

B **Where can you wear the clothes in A? Put a ✗ in the correct box.**
Wo können Sie die Kleidung in **A** anziehen? Kreuzen Sie an.

	a party	college	a job interview	a friend's house
1.	☐	☐	☐	☐
2.	☐	☐	☐	☐
3.	☐	☐	☐	☐
4.	☐	☐	☐	☐
5.	☐	☐	☐	☐

C **Tell your partner what you think.**
Partnerarbeit. Was meinen Sie?

Example: **I think you can wear the clothes in 2 to a friend's house.**

2 Colours and clothes

A What are the colours? Write them down.
Wie heißen die Farben? Schreiben Sie sie auf.

green black red white blue yellow brown

cklba 1. ______	neerg 4. ______	thiew 6. ______
uleb 2. ______	edr 5. ______	lowley 7. ______
wornb 3. ______		

B Talk to a partner. Are the clothes in the photos cool?
Partnerarbeit. Finden Sie die Kleidung auf den Fotos cool?

Example: **Do you like the white trousers? – Yes, I do. / No, I don't.**

C Read the dialogue.
Lesen Sie den Dialog.

Paula: Do you like the colour of the skirt?
Jane: Yes, I do. I like blue.
Paula: Does it go with my top?
Jane: Yes, it does. Blue and white look good together.

D And your clothes? Ask a partner.
Partnerarbeit. Fragen Sie, ob Ihre Kleidung zusammenpasst.

Examples:
Student A: **Do you like the colour of my jacket?**
Student B: **Yes, I do. I like black.**
Student A: **Does it go with my jeans?**
Student B: **Yes, it does. Black and blue look good together.**

3 The right clothes?

A Listen to the CD. Complete the sentence.
Hören Sie die CD an. Vervollständigen Sie den Satz.

John is on the way to ______________________.

B Listen to the CD. John has got a letter. Number the things in the order you hear them.
Hören Sie die CD an. Nummerieren Sie die Gegenstände in der Reihenfolge, in der Sie sie hören.

C What helps you at an interview? Complete the questions.
Was hilft Ihnen bei einem Vorstellungsgespräch? Vervollständigen Sie die Fragen.

1. Does nice hair help at an interview?
2. Do clean shoes help ______________?
3. __________ a tattoo help ______________?
4. __________ a piercing ______________?
5. __________ a nice jacket ______________?
6. __________ cigarettes ______________?
7. __________ clean trousers ______________?
8. __________ a disco shirt ______________?

D Ask a partner the questions in exercise C. Your partner answers.
Partnerarbeit. Stellen Sie die Fragen in Aufgabe C. Ihre Partnerin / Ihr Partner antwortet.

Examples: **Does ... help? – Yes, it does. / No, it doesn't.**
Do ... help? – Yes, they do. / No, they don't.

4 You cannot always be cool!

T9 **A Read the letter to a magazine and the answer.**
Lesen Sie den Leserbrief und die Antwort darauf.

Dear Amanda,

I've got a problem. It's stupid really but I often think about it. It's hard to always be cool. I've got some great new jeans. I think I look cool in them, but my friends say they aren't cool now. They're too old – three months!

I've got some really cool make-up. It looks great when I go to discos or to parties. But my teacher always says, "It isn't OK for college or for job interviews!"

In the evening my friend and I don't meet our friends. We watch *Megahits*, our favourite TV programme. The DJ is great. I like him. And his programme makes us really cool!

It's so hard to be cool. What can I do?

Best wishes,
Sally

Don't try so hard to be cool. That isn't cool!
Amanda

B Answer the questions. Underline the right answer.
Beantworten Sie die Fragen. Unterstreichen Sie die richtige Antwort.

1. What does Sally often think about? (Her jeans. / Her problem.)
2. What has Sally got? (Some new jeans. / A new top.)
3. How old are her jeans? (One month. / Three months.)
4. Does the teacher like Sally's make-up? (Yes, she does. / No, she doesn't.)
5. Who does Sally watch *Megahits* with? (Her parents. / Her friend.)
6. What does Amanda say? (Always be cool. / Don't try so hard.)

C And you? Choose a cool slogan or think of a new slogan.
Suchen Sie einen coolen Spruch aus oder denken Sie sich einen neuen Spruch aus.

My favourite slogan is: ______________________________

5 Practice page

A What are the questions? Put the words in the right order.
Wie lauten die Fragen? Bringen Sie die Wörter in die richtige Reihenfolge.

1. wear/you/Do/clothes/nice/? Do you wear nice clothes?
2. drive/you/Do/a/car/nice/? ______
3. like/cool/music/you/Do/? ______
4. you/watch/cool/TV programmes/Do/? ______
5. meet/Do/lots of/nice/you/people/? ______
6. go to/Do/cool/discos/you/? ______

B Complete the sentences with do or does.
Vervollständigen Sie die Sätze mit **do** oder **does**.

1. Do you know him?
2. ______ his parents live here?
3. ______ he live with his parents?
4. ______ you know where he lives?
5. ______ he go to college?

C Complete the sentences. Use some of the words in the box.
Vervollständigen Sie die Sätze. Benutzen Sie einige Wörter aus dem Kasten.

1. Our parents can't always help us with English.
2. He's John. I like ______ and ______ sister.
3. Where's ______ new CD? Have you got it with ______?
4. I meet my friends and ______ girlfriends every day.
5. ______ friend often helps me at college.
6. Here's Tina. Can you help ______ with ______ books?

I	me	my
you	you	your
he	him	his
she	her	her
we	~~us~~	our
they	them	their

D Number the sentences. Look at the letter on page 20 for help.
Nummerieren Sie die Sätze. Schauen Sie den Brief auf Seite 20 an.

- [ ] What can I do?
- [ ] Dear Amanda,
- [2] My friends don't like my clothes.
- [ ] Robert
- [ ] Best wishes,
- [ ] But I think my clothes are OK.

6 Check your English

A Take the test. Ask the questions in English.
Wie fragen Sie jemanden, …

1. ob er/sie Fußball spielt? ______
2. ob seine/ihre Eltern hier wohnen? ______
3. ob sein/ihr Bruder Motorrad fährt? ______
4. ob ihm/ihr Ihr T-Shirt gefällt? ______
5. was er/sie von der Farbe hält? ______
6. ob Ihr T-Shirt zu Ihrer Hose passt? ______
7. ob saubere Schuhe bei einem Vorstellungsgespräch helfen? ______
______
8. ob Schwarz seine/ihre Lieblingsfarbe ist? ______

B Draw the correct number of icons in the circles.
Malen Sie die richtige Anzahl an Smilies in die Kreise.

☺☺☺ Kann ich schon! ☺☺ Kann ich ein bisschen! ☺ Kann ich bald!

1. Ich kann fragen, was jemand (oft) macht. ○○○

2. Ich kann fragen, ob jemand etwas mag. ○○○

3. Ich kann Farben benennen. ○○○

4. Ich kann Kleidungsstücke benennen. ○○○

Simple present – questions   Gegenwart – Fragen

Frage		Frage	
Do I	speak English?	Does he	look cool?
Do you		Does she	
Do we		Does it	
Do you			
Do they			

Positive Aussage	Frage	Positive Aussage	Frage
I go to college.	Do I go to college?	He likes CDs.	Does he like CDs?
You speak English.	Do you speak English?	She plays tennis.	Does she play tennis?
We try hard.	Do we try hard?	It watches TV.	Does it watch TV?
They watch TV.	Do they watch TV?		

Anwendung
In der 3. Person Singular wird die Frage mit **does** gebildet.
Beispiel: Does Sarah speak English?

Problems 4

1 Sam and the months of the year

A Sam has got problems with everything! He is never happy!
Look at the photos and read the texts.
Schauen Sie die Fotos an und lesen Sie die Texte.

In January it is too cold.
It snows too much in February.

It's too windy in March.
It rains too much in April.

In May he gets hayfever.
It's too sunny in June.

It's too hot in July.
Sam's friends are on holiday in August.

It's too cloudy in September.
It's foggy in October.

The days are too short in November.
The shops are too full in December.

B Talk to a partner about the months of the year.
Partnerarbeit. Sagen Sie welcher Monat Ihnen gefällt und welcher Monat nicht.

Example: **I like June because I like hot weather.**
I don't like January because it's too cold.
My favourite month is December.

2 Richard's problems

A Sam is talking to his friend Richard Watson. Read the dialogue.

Richard: Where were you yesterday?
Sam: I was in college. How was your day yesterday?
Richard: It was bad. I was really angry with my brother. When I arrived home, he was in my room.

B Act dialogues with a partner. Use the words in the boxes.

Example: **Student A: Where were you yesterday?**
Student B: I was at college.

yesterday on Friday
last weekend last week

in Stuttgart at college at the cinema
at the shops at the doctor's at a party

C Act dialogues with a partner. Use the words under the photos.

Example: **Student A: It was a bad day for me yesterday.**
Student B: What was the problem?
Student A: I was ill.

ill

late for college

tired all day

angry with my mum and dad

unhappy

D Richard was angry with his brother in exercise A. What did he do?
Match the verbs with the correct nouns in your exercise book.
Richard war sauer auf seinen Bruder in Aufgabe A. Was hat er angestellt? Ordnen Sie die Verben zu den richtigen Nomen in Ihrem Heft.

opened looked at used
watched listened to played with

TV computer games laptop
books computer CDs

E Now make sentences with the verbs and nouns in D.

Example: **Richard's brother opened his laptop.**

3 Sam's problems

A Listen to the CD. Who was angry with Sam?

His ______________________________

B Listen to the CD again. Did Joanne do it or not? Put a ✗ in the correct box.
Hören Sie die CD noch einmal an. Kreuzen Sie „Yes" oder „No" an.

	Yes, she did.	No, she didn't.
1. Did Joanne phone Sam?	☒	☐
2. Did she shout at him?	☐	☐
3. Did she ask him lots of questions?	☐	☐
4. Did she say he was great?	☐	☐
5. Did she use bad words?	☐	☐
6. Did she listen to Sam?	☐	☐

C Sam did not help Joanne when she was on holiday. Listen to the CD. Number the pictures in the order you hear them on the CD.

D What didn't Sam do? Complete the sentences.

1. Sam didn't meet his girlfriend Joanne.
2. He didn't ______________________ her father.
3. He ______________________ phone Joanne on holiday.
4. He ______________ look after ______________.
5. He ______________________ chocolates for Joanne.

4 Wendy's new friend

T12 **A** **Read the story about Wendy and her new friend, Sarah.**

Wendy Jones arrived home from college. She didn't look very happy. She went to her room and listened to a CD. Her mum knew that there was a problem. She went to Wendy's room.

"Are you OK?" Mrs Jones asked. Wendy looked at her mum and Mrs Jones saw that Wendy was not OK.

"You can always talk to me," said Mrs Jones.

"A new girl arrived at the college last month. Her name is Sarah."

"What's the problem?" asked Mrs Jones.

"We went to the disco last Saturday. Sarah took happy pills. I said she was stupid. So she didn't talk to me for two days.

Then on Saturday we went to the shops. Sarah took a top and didn't pay for it. I said she was stupid again. So she didn't talk to me again."

"That wasn't nice!" said Wendy's mum.

"Then today in college I saw her with Paul Lee from my class. She kissed him. She knows that I like him. I said she wasn't a good friend and then I came home. I did everything wrong, Mum!"

"Wrong? You did everything right," said Mrs Jones. "That girl really wasn't a good friend. – Oh, Paul phoned. Can you go to the college disco with him on Saturday …?"

B **Answer the questions on the text.**

1. Who arrived home from college? Wendy ______.
2. What did Wendy do in her room? ______.
3. Who went to Wendy's room? ______.
4. What did Sarah take at the disco? ______.
5. What did Sarah take in the shop? ______.
6. Who did Sarah kiss? ______.
7. Who went home? ______.
8. What is on Saturday? ______.

5 Practice page

A Put in the correct form of the verb.
Ergänzen Sie die richtige Form des Verbs.

1. It (be) was a very cold day in December.
2. Pete (go) ________ to college.
3. He (see) ________ his friend Tom.
4. He (talk) ________ to Tom.
5. Tom (help) ________ him with the test.
6. But Tom **and** Pete (be) ______ very bad!

B Jane always has a great time at discos. And her friend Anne?
Complete the sentences with the negative form of the verb.

	Jane	Anne
1.	I liked the evening at the disco.	I didn't like the evening at the disco.
2.	I saw nice boys there.	I ____________________ nice boys there.
3.	I liked the music.	I ____________________ the music.
4.	I talked to lots of my friends.	I ____________________ to lots of my friends.
5.	I used my mobile.	I ____________________ my mobile.
6.	I walked home with a nice boy.	I ____________________ home with a nice boy.

C Andy has a problem. Put the words in the right order.

1. the bus / did you / see / ?
   Did you see the bus?
2. the motorbike / see / Did you / ?
   ____
3. pills / take / Did you / happy / ?
   ____
4. your parents / Did you / about the car / ask / ?
   ____
5. your mobile / in the car / use / Did you / ?
   ____

D Which word is wrong?
Welches Wort passt nicht zu den anderen? Unterstreichen Sie es.

1. Saturday, September, November, October
2. January, June, Friday, February
3. looked, watched, help, talked
4. went, had, go, saw

6 Check your English

A **Take the test. Write the sentences in English.**
Schreiben Sie die Sätze auf Englisch.

1. Ich war gestern in der Disko. I was at the disco yesterday.
2. Unser Lehrer war gestern sauer. ____________
3. Sam hat gestern Musik gehört. ____________
4. Joanne hat nicht Fußball gespielt. ____________
5. Juli ist mein Lieblingsmonat. ____________
6. Warst du gestern in der Berufsschule? ____________
7. Hast du gestern ferngesehen? ____________

B **Draw the correct number of icons in the circles.**
Malen Sie die richtige Anzahl an Smilies in die Kreise.

☺☺☺ Kann ich schon! ☺☺ Kann ich ein bisschen! ☺ Kann ich bald!

1. Ich kann sagen, wo jemand war. ○○○
2. Ich kann sagen, wo jemand nicht war. ○○○
3. Ich kann sagen, was jemand getan hat. ○○○
4. Ich kann sagen, was jemand nicht getan hat. ○○○
5. Ich kann fragen, ob jemand etwas getan hat. ○○○
6. Ich kann die Monate benennen. ○○○

Simple present, Simple past Gegenwart, Einfache Vergangenheit

► **Regelmäßige Verben**

Positive Aussage	Verneinung	Frage
I play football.	I don't play tennis.	Do you play basketball?
I played football yesterday.	I didn't play (did not play) tennis.	Did you play basketball?

► **Unregelmäßige Verben**

Positive Aussage	Verneinung	Frage
I go to college.	I don't go by bus.	Do you go by car?
I went to the disco yesterday.	I didn't go by bus.	Did you go by car?

Unregelmäßige Verben haben besondere Formen für die positive Aussage.
Siehe Liste auf S. 47.

► **to be, was / were**

Positive Aussage	Verneinung	Frage
I am at college today.	I'm not in my room.	Are you at home now?
I was at the disco yesterday.	I wasn't in my brother's room.	Were you at home last night?

Music and media

5

1 Media and me

A **Do the media quiz. Put a ✗ in the correct box.**
Machen Sie das Medienquiz. Kreuzen Sie an.

1

- ☐ **a)** I never go to the cinema.
- ☐ **b)** I sometimes go to the cinema.
- ☐ **c)** I often go to the cinema.

2

- ☐ **a)** I never watch DVDs.
- ☐ **b)** I sometimes watch DVDs.
- ☐ **c)** I often watch DVDs.

3

- ☐ **a)** I never use chat rooms.
- ☐ **b)** I sometimes use chat rooms.
- ☐ **c)** I love chatting.

4

- ☐ **a)** I don't like watching TV.
- ☐ **b)** I like watching TV.
- ☐ **c)** I love watching TV.

5

- ☐ **a)** I don't like listening to music.
- ☐ **b)** I like listening to music.
- ☐ **c)** I love listening to music.

B **Give points for each answer.**
Points: a = 0, b = 1, c = 2.
What kind of media person are you?
Vergeben Sie Punkte für jede Antwort.
Punkte: a = 0, b = 1, c = 2.
Interessieren Sie sich für Medien?

0–4	You aren't a media person. Wake up! This is the 21st century!
5–7	You're sometimes a media person.
8–10	Yes, you're a media person. But have you got time for other things?

C **Talk to a partner about media.**
Example: **I often watch TV but I never use chat rooms.**

2 My media, your media

A **Tim is at college with his friend Christine. Read the dialogue.**

Tim: Hey, Christine. I want to read about the Sugababes. Can I borrow your magazine?
Christine: OK. But you must give it back.
Tim: OK. Thanks, Christine.
Christine: Bye, Tim. See you later.

B **Make dialogues like the one in A. Use the words in the boxes.**

Example: **Student A: I want to send a text to my mum. Can I borrow your mobile?**
Student B: OK, but you must give it back in a minute.

want	borrow
read about my favourite football team	a pen
write a telephone number	a euro
take a photo of you and me	your magazine
buy a bus ticket	your mobile
send a text to my mum	your sports magazine
read something	your mobile

C **What do they want to buy? Finish the sentences. Use the words in the box.**

mobile phone laptop DVD player TV

1. Bill does projects for college. He wants to buy a ______________________.
2. Judy has got lots of friends. She ______________________.
3. Joe likes soaps. He ______________________.
4. Sharon and Frank watch lots of films. They ______________________.

D **Ask a partner what he / she likes doing on the computer.**
Partnerarbeit. Was machen Sie am liebsten am Computer?

Example: **Student A: What do you like doing on the computer?**
Student B: I like chatting.
Student A: I like chatting, too. or **I don't like chatting.**

chatting reading emails writing emails
downloading music looking at websites
reading blogs writing blogs playing games

Blog – Online-Tagebuch

3 Time for texting

A Listen to the CD. Which dialogue (a – d) goes with which text?
Hören Sie die CD an. Welcher Dialog (a – d) passt zu welcher SMS?

GR8 = great	SRY = sorry
CU2MORO = See you tomorrow.	LOL = lots of love
PLS = please	RU OK = Are you OK?
THX = thanks	

B Carol is at Sue's house. Listen to the CD. Put a ✗ in the correct box.

	Yes	No
1. Does *Soft Radio* play new songs?	☐	☒
2. Does Sue like some old songs?	☐	☐
3. Do Carol's parents listen to lots of old songs?	☐	☐
4. Is Carol's boyfriend with the two girls?	☐	☐
5. Does Carol like the song, *Daniel*?	☐	☐
6. Does she want to send the song to her boyfriend?	☐	☐

4 Girl groups: Here today, here tomorrow too?

T15 **A Read the article.**

What's the most famous girl group? The Spice Girls, of course. But where are they now? Some of the girls have solo careers but they don't sing together any more. Other girl groups come and go, too: All Saints, Thunderbugs and Atomic Kitten.

The Sugababes are also a girl group. They became famous with "One Touch", "Angels with Dirty Faces" and "Three". But the group that sang "Overload" in 2001 wasn't the group that sang "Red Dress" five years later.

In 2000 three girls came together to make music: Keisha Buchanan, Mutya Buena and Siobhan Donaghy. They knew each other from school. And the big difference to the Spice Girls was that they wrote their songs. Their first single, "Overload", was a big hit all over the world. But then in 2001 Siobhan decided to leave the Sugababes. Heidi Range, ex-Atomic Kitten, was the new Sugababe.

The band made more hit CDs. Then in 2005 there were rumours that Heidi wanted to start a solo career. Mutya had a baby and left the band. One day later the Sugababes' manager had the answer: a new Sugababe, Amelle Berrabah. She sang on the new single, "Red Dress". And then Heidi wanted to stay in the band after all!

In 2000 the Sugababes were Keisha, Mutya and Siobhan. In 2002 they were Keisha, Mutya and Heidi. In 2005 they were Keisha, Heidi and Amelle. And today? And tomorrow?

B Tell the story of the Sugababes. Put the sentences in the order of the text and number them.
Ordnen Sie die Sätze nach der Reihenfolge im Text. Schreiben Sie die Nummern in die Kästchen.

- [ ] Mutya had a baby and left the group.
- [ ] Siobhan left the group.
- [1] There were other girl groups before the Sugababes.
- [ ] The Sugababes came together in 2000.
- [ ] Amelle was the new Sugababe on "Red Dress".
- [ ] Their first single was "Overload".

Cut out the cards and ask your partner questions. Your partner has to give one of the answers on the back of the card.
Schneiden Sie die Karten aus und stellen Sie Ihrem Partner / Ihrer Partnerin Fragen. Er / Sie muss eine der Antworten geben, die auf der Rückseite Ihrer Karte steht.

Are you a  fan?

Do you and your family speak  at home?

Have we got  on Monday?

Have you got a  ?

Are you from  ?

Have your parents got a  ?

Do you ride a  ?

Do you like  clothes?

Have you got a  ?

Is  your favourite colour?

Has your mother got a  ?

Is your car  ?

Is your teacher from  ?

Has your mother got  hair?

Do you play  ?

Does your dad often watch soaps? 

Does your friend play  ?

Does your mother listen to pop  ?

Do your friends often go to the 

?

Do your parents speak  ?

Yes, we do. / No, we don't.	Yes, I am. / No, I'm not.
Yes, I have. / No, I haven't.	Yes, we have. / No, we haven't.
Yes, they have. / No, they haven't.	Yes, I am. / No, I'm not.
Yes, I do. / No, I don't.	Yes, I do. / No, I don't.
Yes, it is. / No, it isn't.	Yes, I have. / No, I haven't.
Yes, it is. / No, it isn't.	Yes, she has. / No, she hasn't.
Yes, she has. / No, she hasn't.	Yes, he/she is. / No, he/she isn't.
Yes, he does. / No, he doesn't.	Yes, I do. / No, I don't.
Yes, she does. / No, she doesn't.	Yes, he/she does. / No, he/she doesn't.
Yes, they do. / No, they don't.	Yes, they do. / No, they don't.

Killer on Mulligan Street

Elinor Winter, 83, was killed in her house last Monday

Read what Mr and Mrs Fitzgerald, Mr and Mrs Simmons, Meg Winter and the postman told the police. Cut out the sentences and put them in the right order. Start with Monday morning.
When you finish, turn the paper around and you will get a picture of the killer.

Mr and Mrs Fitzgerald

Mr and Mrs Simmons

Meg Winter

the postman

Lesen Sie, was Mrs und Mr Fitzgerald, Mr und Mrs Simmons, Meg Winter und der Postbote der Polizei erzählt haben.

jacket in Mrs Winter's garden at ten past ten. Meg Winter phoned her grandmother at quarter past ten. They talked for thirty

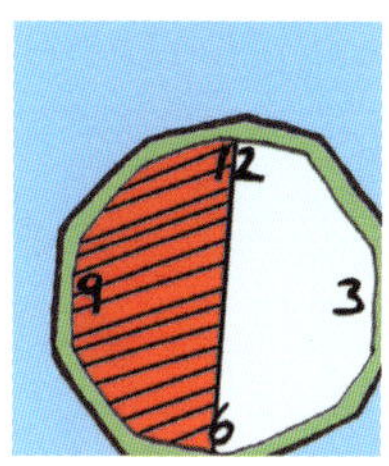

to eleven. Mrs Winter didn't open the door. Mrs Simmons went to the

Mrs Winter on the floor."
Mrs Winter was dead.
Mrs Simmons phoned the police.

THE END

minutes. Mrs Fitzgerald went to Mrs Winter's house at five

MONDAY MORNING

Mrs Fitzgerald: "I got up at six o'clock. I saw a light in Mrs Winter's house."
Mr Fitzgerald: "I left my

Mrs Fitzgerald.
Mrs Simmons: "I came from the post office at twenty past eleven. I looked at Mrs Winter's house. The door was open. The

post office at five past eleven. A man in a black jacket came out of Mrs Winter's garden. At ten past eleven Mrs Winter phoned

door was open."
Mrs Simmons: "Mrs Winter's door was open at twenty to twelve. I went into the house. I saw

house at half past six. Mrs Winter was at her door."
Mr Simmons saw a man in a black

postman was at the door." The postman said: "I went to Mrs Winter's house at half past eleven. Mrs Winter was not there but the

5 Practice page

A What do the people like doing? Make sentences.

1. Frank/watch horror films Frank likes watching horror films.
2. Paula/read music magazines ______.
3. Tina/watch music DVDs ______.
4. Mark/send texts ______.
5. Helen/chat on the internet ______.
6. Rod/listen to rap music ______.

B What do the people in A want to do next weekend? Use the words in the box.

look for a DVD in a DVD shop | go to the cinema | buy a new mobile phone
burn a CD with ~~/ favourite~~ songs | buy *Top Hits* | go to an internet café

1. Frank wants to ______.
2. Paula wants to ______.
3. Tina wants to ______.
4. Mark wants to ______.
5. Helen wants to ______.
6. Rod wants to burn a CD with his favourite songs.

C Andrew is visiting the Steinle family in Stuttgart. What does Mr Steinle say?

Was sagt Herr Steinle zu Andrew? Schreiben Sie die Sätze auf Englisch.

1. Willst du fernsehen? Do you want to watch television?
2. Ich liebe es fernzusehen. ______
3. Du kannst hier sitzen. ______
4. Hörst du gern Musik? ______
5. Was machst du gern am Computer? ______
6. Willst du jetzt gehen? ______

D Underline the correct answers.

Unterstreichen Sie die richtigen Antworten.

1. Here's your CD. – Thanks./Please.
2. Can you help me, please? – No, I can't. Sorry./No, please.
3. Bye, Paul. – Hi, John./Bye, John.
4. Do you want to borrow my CD? – Yes, please./Yes, thanks.

6 Check your English

A How do you say the following sentences in English?
Wie drücken Sie Folgendes auf Englisch aus?

1. Er spielt gern Fußball. ______________________.
2. Sie liest nicht gern Bücher. ______________________.
3. Ich liebe es, Zeitschriften zu lesen. ______________________.
4. Meine Freunde wollen jetzt gehen. ______________________.
5. Du musst mich besuchen. ______________________.
6. Kann ich deinen Kugelschreiber ausleihen? ______________________.

B Draw the correct number of icons in the circles.
Malen Sie die richtige Anzahl an Smilies in die Kreise.

☺☺☺ Kann ich schon! ☺☺ Kann ich ein bisschen! ☺ Kann ich bald!

1. Ich kann sagen, was ich gern tue. ○○○
2. Ich kann sagen, was ich nicht gern tue. ○○○
3. Ich kann sagen, was ich sehr gern tue. ○○○
4. Ich kann sagen, was ich tun will. ○○○
5. Ich kann sagen, was jemand tun muss. ○○○
6. Ich kann jemanden bitten, mir etwas zu leihen. ○○○

I Verb + gerund (-ing form) Verb + Gerundium (-ing-Form)

► **to like / to love**

Positive Aussage	Verneinung
I like going to the disco.	I don't like helping him.
He loves playing football.	

II Modal verbs + infinitive Modalverben + Grundform

► **can**

Positive Aussage	Verneinung	Frage
I can speak English.	Kelly can't play football.	Can you burn a CD?

► **must**

Positive Aussage
I must go now.

III want to + infinitive

Positive Aussage	Verneinung
I want to meet the new teacher.	I don't want to go.

A place to live 6

1 Town and country

A What's in the town in the picture? Use the words in the box.

Example: There's a factory. There are houses. There are …

bridge
church
cinema
disco
factory
farms
fields
houses
park
river
roads
shops
station
village
wood

B What's in the country? Use the words in the box.

C Write the words from the box in the correct part of the circles.
Schreiben Sie die Wörter im Kasten in die richtigen Teile der Kreise.

town and country

town

country

park

church

fields

2 I'm bored in the country!

A Pat is phoning her friends. Read the dialogue.

Pat: Hi, Bill. What are you doing at the moment?
Bill: I'm sitting in my room. I'm using my computer. It's great.
Pat: And I'm bored! Bye, Bill.

Pat: Hi, Sally. What are you doing now?
Sally: I'm working for college.
Pat: OK. Bye, Sally.

Pat: Hi, Jill. What are you doing?
Jill: I'm reading a magazine, the new *Top Hits*.
Pat: OK. Bye, Jill.

B Act dialogues with a partner. Choose one of the pictures below.
Partnerarbeit. Wählen Sie eins der Bilder unten.

Example: **Student A: Hi, ... What are you doing at the moment?**
Student B: I'm watching TV.
Student A: OK. Bye, ...

watching TV

reading a book

shopping

talking to a friend

writing an email

doing homework

C Pat is phoning her friend Debbie in London. Read the dialogue.

Pat: Tell me about your new home.
Debbie: It's a flat.
Pat: What's it near?
Debbie: It's near the shops and a big cinema.
Pat: It sounds great!

D Ask a partner about his / her home. Look at exercise C for help.

3 In the town

A **Listen to the CD. What's near Debbie's flat? Mark (✗) the correct photos.**
Hören Sie die CD an. Was ist in der Nähe von Debbies Wohnung? Kreuzen Sie die richtigen Fotos an.

B **Listen to the CD. Pat and Debbie are talking about their plans for next month. Draw lines to put the sentence halves together.**
Hören Sie die CD an. Pat und Debbie besprechen ihre Pläne für den kommenden Monat. Verbinden Sie die richtigen Satzhälften.

1. They're meeting	**a)** football in the park on Tuesday.
2. They're playing	**b)** in bed late on Saturday!
3. They're visiting	**c)** Debbie's boyfriend on Wednesday.
4. They're looking for	**d)** new clothes in the big shops on Thursday.
5. They're going to	**e)** Debbie's friends on Monday.
6. They're staying	**f)** the disco on Friday.

C **Listen again and check your answers in exercise B.**
Hören Sie die CD noch einmal an. Prüfen Sie Ihre Antworten.

D **What are you doing next week? Tell a partner.**

Example:
Student A: What are you doing next week?
Student B: I'm meeting friends on Sunday.

Das **present continuous** drückt aus, was man fest geplant oder vereinbart hat. Eine Zeitangabe (next week, tomorrow afternoon, on Saturday, …) ist oft dabei.

4 From the country to the town

T18 **A Read the text.**

Pat is in the train. She is going from her home in the country to London. She's reading the new *Young Girl* magazine.

▶ There are lots of problems in towns for young people. There are people who do bad things. They sell drugs to young people, or they steal their mobiles and their money.

Towns are exciting, but they aren't healthy places to live. There are factories, lots of cars, and lots of young people smoke there.

And there aren't jobs for all the young people. Some of them get bored and do stupid things. They steal cars or things from shops.

And don't go into a town late on Friday or Saturday evening! There are lots of drunken people. Stay at home or go to the country!

Pat's mobile is ringing. It's Debbie.
"Hi, Pat," she says. "I'm reading the new *Young Girl*."
"Yes," says Pat. "There's an article …"
"… about towns," says Debbie. "I know. I just want to tell you not to worry. I can look after you. OK?"
"Yes," says Pat. "I'm not really worried."
"Good," says Debbie. "Mum is cooking this evening. What do you want to eat?"
"Nothing too exciting, please! Bye!"

B Mark the sentences true or false. Put a ✗ in the correct box.

	True	False
1. Bad people sell magazines to young people.	☐	☒
2. There are jobs for all young people in towns.	☐	☐
3. There are lots of drunken people in towns on Friday and Saturday.	☐	☐
4. Pat phones Debbie.	☐	☐
5. Pat isn't really worried.	☐	☐
6. Debbie's dad is cooking this evening.	☐	☐

5 Practice page

A People in a town: What are they doing at the moment? Put in the correct form of the verb.
Ergänzen Sie die richtige Form des Verbs.

1. Meg is a policewoman. She (talk) ______________ to a tourist.
2. Joanna and Gale are (look after) ______________ old people.
3. Greg (cook) ______________ for people without a home.
4. Bill (work) ______________ in a hospital.
5. Kate and Frank (help) ______________ some young people.
6. Tom and Ricky (clean) ______________ the youth club.

B College time: What are they saying? Put the words in the right order.
Bringen Sie die Wörter in die richtige Reihenfolge.

1. to the disco / I'm / this evening / not going
   I'm not going to the disco this evening.
2. tonight / aren't watching / the late film / We / on TV
   ______________.
3. My friends / me / in town / aren't meeting
   ______________.
4. My teacher / friends / in May / isn't visiting / in England
   ______________.
5. playing / tonight / computer games / I'm not
   ______________.

C Email time: Sabine is writing to her English boyfriend. Silke is helping her. What does Silke say?

1. Wohin gehst du am Wochenende? Where are you going at the weekend?
2. Spielt deine Mannschaft heute? ______________
3. Triffst du Paul heute Abend? ______________
4. Gehst du morgen in die Disko? ______________
5. Was machst du heute Nachmittag? ______________
6. Denkst du an mich? ______________

6 Check your English

A Take the test. How do you say the following?
Wie sagen Sie, dass …

1. Sie (gerade) in Ihrem Zimmer sitzen? ______
2. Sie (gerade) nicht Fußball spielen? ______
3. Pat morgen in die Stadt fährt? ______
4. es einen Park in der Nähe von Ihrer Wohnung gibt? ______
5. es viele Autos in der Stadt gibt? ______

Wie fragen Sie jemanden, …

6. was er/sie (gerade) macht? ______
7. ob er/sie seinen/ihren Eltern morgen hilft? ______

B Draw the correct number of icons in the circles.
Malen Sie die richtige Anzahl an Smilies in die Kreise.

☺☺☺ Kann ich schon! ☺☺ Kann ich ein bisschen! ☺ Kann ich bald!

1. Ich kann sagen, was ich gerade mache. ○○○
2. Ich kann sagen, was ich nicht mache. ○○○
3. Ich kann sagen, was ich morgen mache. ○○○
4. Ich kann fragen, ob jemand etwas macht. ○○○
5. Ich kann sagen, was es in der Stadt gibt. ○○○
6. Ich kann sagen, was in der Nähe von meinem Zuhause ist. ○○○

I there is / there are

Positive Aussage	Verneinung	Frage
There's a disco in our road.	There isn't a supermarket.	Is there a cinema?
There are some people in the park.	There aren't any boys.	Are there any girls?

II Present continuous Verlaufsform der Gegenwart

Positive Aussage	Verneinung	Frage
I'm reading	I'm not playing	Am I helping?
You're reading	You aren't playing	Are you helping?
He's / She's / It's reading	He / She / It isn't playing	Is he / she / it helping?
We're reading	We aren't playing	Are we helping?
You're reading	You aren't playing	Are you helping?
They're reading	They aren't playing	Are they helping?

Anwendung

1. Handlungen, die im Moment stattfinden: I'm watching TV now.
2. Zukünftige Handlungen mit Zeitangabe: I'm going to town tomorrow. My sister isn't coming with me. Are you playing football tomorrow afternoon? – No, I'm not.

Different culture, different people 7

1 My food, your food

A **Lots of people like food from other countries. Talk about this food from other countries. Use the words in the box.**

England Italy Russia
Spain Turkey the USA

Example: **I think that popcorn comes from the USA.**

1. popcorn

3. doner kebab

5. paella

2. fish and chips

4. beef stroganoff

6. spaghetti Bolognese

B **Talk to a partner about food.**

Examples: **Do you like spaghetti Bolognese? – Yes, I do. / No, I don't.**
What's your favourite food? – . . .

C **Write the correct languages and countries in the table.**
Vervollständigen Sie die Tabelle mit den richtigen Sprachen und Ländern.

Country	Language
England	________
________	Italian
________	Russian
________	Spanish
________	Turkish
USA	________
Germany	________

2 Help with problems

A Mr Hunt, a teacher at Westside College, is talking to a student. Read the dialogue.

Mr Hunt: What's the problem, Paul? You look unhappy.
Paul: The students in my class don't talk to me. They don't understand me.
Mr Hunt: I'll organise extra English lessons for you.
Paul: Will English lessons help?
Mr Hunt: Yes, they will. The students will understand you better. Things won't be so hard.

B Match the sentences.

1. I can't find my English book.
2. I'm hungry.
3. I have a job interview on Monday.
4. I can't do exercise 4.
5. I want to phone my mum.
6. I haven't got enough money for the cinema.

a) I'll read the question. We'll work on it together.
b) I'll help you to look for it.
c) We'll watch TV at my house.
d) I'll lend you my mobile for two minutes.
e) I'll make spaghetti Bolognese.
f) I'll help you to get ready for it.

C Act out dialogues with the sentences in B.

Example: Student A: What's the problem?
Student B: I can't find my book.
Student A: I'll help you to look for it.

D What will you do next year? What won't you do? Think of ideas.
Was werden Sie nächstes Jahr (nicht) tun? Denken Sie sich Beispiele aus.

Things you will do:	Things you won't do:
I will work hard at college.	I won't smoke.

3 Let's have a party!

A Listen to the CD. Match the photos to the festivals in the box.

Festivals

- ☐ Halloween
- ☐ Bonfire Night
- ☐ St Patrick's Day
- ☐ Thanksgiving

B Listen to the CD again. Fill in the information about the festivals.

Festival	When is it?	What do people do?
St Patrick's Day		
Thanksgiving		
Halloween		
Bonfire Night		

C Listen to the CD. Write the correct letters (a–d) in the boxes.

D Listen to the CD again. Match the countries in the box with the photos in exercise C.

a) ____________ c) ____________

b) ____________ d) ____________

Australia Canada
New Zealand Scotland

4 Britain in the world, the world in Britain

T21 **A Read the text.**

Britain was once a country where only white people lived. Some of these people left Britain and went all over the world. They went to North America. That's why there are lots of English-speakers in the USA and Canada. And they went to the other side of the world, to Australia and New Zealand. These are still English-speaking countries, but they are now independent from Britain.

Britain once went to the world, now the world comes to Britain. Lots of people from Africa and India live in Britain today. There are 270 different nationalities in London and they speak 250 different languages. A quarter of the people in London are non-white. London has more non-whites than other European capitals.

That's why, in 2012, the world will come to multi-cultural Britain – for the Olympic Games.

B Finish the sentences.
Vervollständigen Sie die Sätze.

1. Britain was once a country where only white people lived.
2. People from Britain went to North ________.
3. All these countries are now ________ from Britain.
4. Lots of people from Africa and ________ live in Britain.
5. London is Britain's ________.
6. The 2012 Olympic ________ will be in Britain.

C Find the six English-speaking countries in the text. Write the countries next to the correct flags.
Finden Sie die sechs englischsprachigen Länder im Text. Schreiben Sie die Ländernamen neben die richtigen Flaggen.

1. ________

2. ________

3. ________

4. ________

5. ________

6. New ________

5 Practice page

A What are they saying? Put the words in the right order.
Bringen Sie die Wörter in die richtige Reihenfolge.

1. buy / for you / I won't / the CD I won't buy the CD for you.
2. go / tomorrow / to the shops / I'll ______.
3. your dog / We'll / look after ______.
4. won't / The teacher / your parents / phone ______.
5. I'll / you / with the exercise / help ______.
6. clean / I'll / the motorbike / for you ______.

B What will happen to Jill? What does Madame Fortuna say?

1. buy / nice car You'll buy a nice car.
2. go / London ______.
3. get / a good job ______.
4. see / a nice boy at a disco ______.
5. have / a baby ______.
6. be / unhappy! ______.

C Madame Fortuna was right! Write the sentences in B in the past tense.
Schreiben Sie die Sätze aus B in der Vergangenheitsform.

1. Jill bought a nice car.
2. She ______ to London.
3. She ______ a good job.
4. She ______.
5. She ______.
6. She ______.

D Complete the puzzle and find the key word.
Vervollständigen Sie das Rätsel und finden Sie das Lösungswort.

1. It's a country on the other side of the world.
2. German – Germany, English – …
3. You're in this country now.
4. It's a "green country".
5. Lots of people came to Britain from Africa and …
6. It's the biggest English-speaking country.
7. Germany – German, Turkey – …

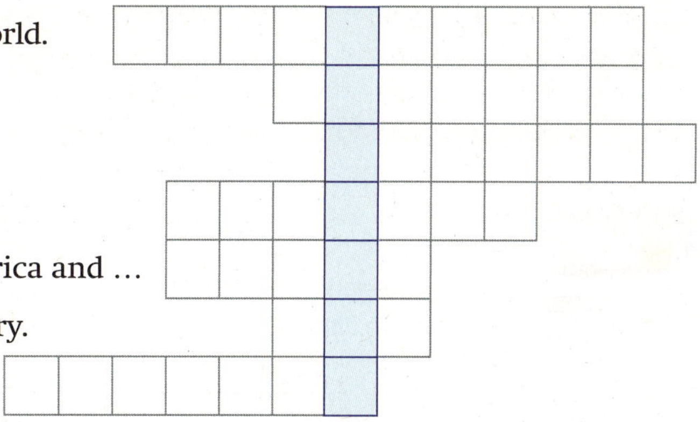

Key word: ______

6 Check your English

A Take the test.
Wie sagen Sie, dass …

1. Sie jemandem helfen werden? ______________________________.
2. Jill nach London gehen wird? ______________________________.
3. Sie nächstes Jahr nicht rauchen werden? ______________________________.
4. Sie ihre Hausaufgaben nicht vergessen werden? ______________________________.
5. die Mannschaft nicht spielen wird? ______________________________.
6. Sie nach Australien fahren werden? ______________________________.
7. Amerikaner an Thanksgiving viel essen? ______________________________.
8. Und wie fragen Sie, ob der Laden morgen öffnen wird? ______________________________

______________________________.

B Draw the correct number of icons in the circles.
Malen Sie die richtige Anzahl an Smilies in die Kreise.

☺☺☺ Kann ich schon! ☺☺ Kann ich ein bisschen! ☺ Kann ich bald!

1. Ich kann Hilfe anbieten. ○○○
2. Ich kann sagen, was geschehen wird. ○○○
3. Ich kann sagen, was nicht geschehen wird. ○○○
4. Ich kann fragen, ob etwas geschehen wird. ○○○
5. Ich kann einige Länder benennen. ○○○
6. Ich kann einige Feste benennen. ○○○

Will-future Zukunft mit will

Positive Aussage		Verneinung		Frage	
I'll (I will)		I won't (I will not)		Will I	
You'll (You will)		You won't (You will not)		Will you	
He'll (He will)		He won't (He will not)		Will he	
She'll (She will)	play	She won't (She will not)	work	Will she	meet Tom?
We'll (We will)		We won't (We will not)		Will we	
You'll (You will)		You won't (You will not)		Will you	
They'll (They will)		They won't (They will not)		Will they	

Anwendung

1. Wenn man Hilfe anbietet: I'll open the door for you.
2. Wenn man einen spontanen Entschluss fasst: Pat? OK, I'll phone her this evening.
3. Wenn man Vermutungen über die Zukunft anstellt: I think the train will be late.

Unregelmäßige Verben

Die Verbformen werden wie folgt aufgeführt: Grundform (infinitive) und einfache Vergangenheit (simple past).

be, was / were	sein
become, became	werden
bring, brought	bringen
buy, bought	kaufen
can, could	können
come, came	kommen
cut, cut	schneiden
drive, drove	fahren
eat, ate	essen
find, found	finden
get, got	erhalten, bekommen
give, gave	geben
go, went	gehen, fahren
have (got), had (got)	haben
know, knew	kennen, wissen
leave, left	verlassen, austreten
lend, lent	leihen
lose, lost	verlieren
make, made	machen
meet, met	(sich) treffen (mit)
must, had to	müssen
put, put	stellen, legen, setzen
read, read	lesen
ride, rode	fahren
ring, rang	klingeln
say, said	sagen
see, saw	sehen
sell, sold	verkaufen
send, sent	senden, verschicken
sing, sang	singen
sit, sat	sitzen
speak, spoke	sprechen
steal, stole	stehlen
take, took	nehmen
tell, told	erzählen
think, thought	denken, meinen
understand, understood	verstehen
wake, woke	aufwachen
wear, wore	(Kleidung) tragen
write, wrote	schreiben

Kapitelbegleitende Wortlisten

Die Übersetzungen beziehen sich auf den jeweiligen Kontext in der angegebenen Unit / Übung.

Abkürzungen und Symbole

AP Activity page
HV Hörverstehensübung
◎ befindet sich auf der Lehrer-Audio-CD
→ siehe Verbform auf Seite 47

Phonetic alphabet Lautschrift

[:] bedeutet, dass der vorangegangene Laut lang ist
['] bedeutet, dass die folgende Silbe eine Hauptbetonung erhält
[ˌ] bedeutet, dass die folgende Silbe eine Nebenbetonung erhält
[‿] bedeutet, dass die beiden Laute miteinander verbunden werden

[i:] meet [mi:t]
[ɑ:] father ['fɑ:ðə]
[ɔ:] morning ['mɔ:niŋ]
[u:] blue [blu:]
[ɜ:] German ['dʒɜ:mən]

[ɪ] in [ɪn]
[e] yes [jes]
[æ] thanks [θæŋks]
[ʌ] much [mʌtʃ]
[ɒ] what [wɒt]
[ʊ] good [gʊd]
[ə] number ['nʌmbə]

[eɪ] name [neɪm]
[aɪ] my [maɪ]
[ɔɪ] boiled [bɔɪld]
[əʊ] phone [fəʊn]
[aʊ] now [naʊ]
[ɪə] hear [hɪə]
[eə] where [weə]
[ʊə] tourist ['tʊərɪst]

[p] pop [pɒp]
[b] bye [baɪ]
[t] town [taʊn]
[d] drink [drɪŋk]
[k] coffee ['kɒfɪ]
[g] good [gʊd]
[tʃ] church [tʃɜ:tʃ]
[dʒ] job [dʒɒb]
[f] fine [faɪn]
[v] very ['verɪ]
[θ] thanks [θæŋks]
[ð] this [ðɪs]

[s] son [sʌn]
[z] is [ɪz]
[ʃ] she [ʃi:]
[ʒ] television [ˌtelɪ'vɪʒn]
[h] he [hi:]
[m] my [maɪ]
[n] now [naʊ]
[ŋ] evening ['i:vnɪŋ]
[l] like ['laɪk]
[r] room [ru:m]
[w] we [wi:]
[y] yes [yes]

Unit 1

1	**about** [ə'baʊt]	über
	and [ænd, ənd]	und
	cool [ku:l]	cool
	England ['ɪŋglənd]	England
	English ['ɪŋglɪʃ]	Engländer/in
	from [frɒm, frəm]	aus, von
	I am (I'm) [aɪ‿æm, aɪm]	ich bin
	me [mi:]	mich, mir
	too [tu:]	auch, zu
1A	**boy** [bɔɪ]	Junge
	girl [gɜ:l]	Mädchen
	he is (he's) [hi:‿ɪz, hi:z]	er ist
	in the photo [ɪn ðə 'fəʊtəʊ]	auf dem Foto
	is [ɪz]	ist
	she is (she's) [ʃi:‿ɪz, ʃi:z]	sie ist
	the [ðɪ, ðə]	der / die / das
1C	**disco** ['dɪskəʊ]	Disko
	music ['mju:zɪk]	Musik
1D	**What's?** [wɒts]	Was ist?
2	**brother** ['brʌðə]	Bruder
	here [hɪə]	hier
	my [maɪ]	mein/e
	sister ['sɪstə]	Schwester
	they are (they're) [ðeɪ‿ɑ:, ðeə]	sie sind
2B	**hi** [haɪ]	Hi
	not [nɒt]	nicht
	yes [jes]	ja
	you are (you're) [ju:‿ɑ:, jɔ:]	du bist, Sie sind, ihr seid
2C	**a** [ə]	ein/e
	now [naʊ]	jetzt
3	**family, families** ['fæməlɪ]	Familie
3A	**CD** [ˌsi:'di:]	CD
◎ HV 3A	**I've got** [aɪv 'gɒt]	ich habe
	one [wʌn, wɒn]	ein/e
	two [tu:]	zwei
3B	**at** [æt, ət]	an
	to **have got** [hæv 'gɒt]	haben
3C	**your** [jɔ:]	dein / Ihr / euer
3D	**book** [bʊk]	Buch
	partner ['pɑ:tnə]	Partner/in
◎ HV 3D	to **look** [lʊk]	schauen
	What have I got? [ˌwɒt‿həv aɪ 'gɒt]	Was habe ich?
3E	**has got** [hæz 'gɒt, həz 'gɒt]	hat
4	**email** ['i:meɪl]	E-Mail
4A	**friend** [frend]	Freund/in
	Best wishes. [ˌbest 'wɪʃɪz]	Alles Gute.
	but [bʌt, bət]	aber
	cat [kæt]	Katze
	college ['kɒlɪdʒ]	Berufs(fach)-schule
	fan [fæn]	Fan
	father ['fɑ:ðə]	Vater
	favourite ['feɪvrɪt]	Lieblings-
	football ['fʊtbɔ:l]	Fußball
	friendly ['frendlɪ]	nett, freundlich
	fun [fʌn]	Spaß
	German ['dʒɜ:mən]	deutsch
	good [gʊd]	gut
	it [ɪt]	es
	job [dʒɒb]	Job
	lots of ['lɒts‿əv]	viel(e)
	mother ['mʌðə]	Mutter
	Mr ['mɪstə]	Herr
	Mrs ['mɪsɪz]	Frau (bei verheirateten Frauen)
	no [nəʊ]	nein; kein
	of [ɒv, əv]	von, bei, aus
	our [aʊə]	unser/e
	parents ['peərənts]	Eltern
	teacher ['ti:tʃə]	Lehrer/in
	team [ti:m]	Team, Mannschaft
	that's [ðæts]	das ist
	there are [ðeər‿ɑ:, ðərə]	es gibt
	there's [ðeəz, ðəz]	es gibt
	this [ðɪs]	diese/r/s
	very ['verɪ]	sehr
	we are (we're) [wi:‿ɑ:, wɪə]	wir sind
	with [wɪð]	mit
4B	**Rachel's** ['reɪtʃəlz]	Rachels
	or [ɔ:]	oder
5A	**Germany** ['dʒɜ:mənɪ]	Deutschland
5B	**number** ['nʌmbə]	Zahl, Nummer
5D	**question** ['kwestʃn]	Frage

Unit 2

1	**free time** [ˌfri: 'taɪm]	Freizeit
	teenager ['ti:nˌeɪdʒə]	Teenager
1A	**computer** [kəm'pju:tə]	Computer
	at six o'clock [ət ˌsɪks‿ə'klɒk]	um sechs Uhr
	car [kɑ:]	Auto
	cinema ['sɪnəmə]	Kino
	to **drive, drove** [draɪv]	fahren
	to **get up, got up** [get 'ʌp, gɒt 'ʌp]	aufstehen
	to **go, went** [gəʊ, went]	gehen, fahren
	to **meet, met** [mi:t, met]	(sich) treffen (mit)
	never ['nevə]	nie(mals)
	often ['ɒftn, 'ɒfn]	oft

Unit 2

	to **play** [pleɪ]	spielen; Sport machen
	to **sit, sat** [sɪt, sæt]	sitzen
	sometimes ['sʌmtaɪmz]	manchmal
	sport [spɔ:t]	Sport
	their [ðeə]	ihr/e
	to [tu:, tʊ, tə]	zu
	to **visit** ['vɪzɪt]	besuchen
	to **watch TV** [wɒtʃ ˌti:'vi:]	fernsehen
2A	**for** [fɔ:, fə]	für
	magazine [ˌmægə'zi:n]	Zeitschrift
	because [bɪ'kɒz, bɪ'kəz]	weil
	game [geɪm]	Spiel
	to **like** [laɪk]	mögen
	motorbike ['məʊtəbaɪk]	Motorrad
	shopping ['ʃɒpɪŋ]	Einkaufen
	to **think, thought** [θɪŋk, θɔ:t]	denken, meinen
	TV soap [ˌti:vi: 'səʊp]	Seifenoper im Fernsehen
	walking ['wɔ:kɪŋ]	Wandern, Spazierengehen
	Who's? [hu:z]	Wer ist?
2C	to **arrive** [ə'raɪv]	ankommen
	half past [ˌhɑ:f 'pɑ:st, ˌhɑ:fpɑ:st ('faɪv)]	halb
	to **leave, left** [li:v, left]	verlassen
	morning ['mɔ:nɪŋ]	Morgen
	quarter past [ˌkwɔ:tə 'pɑ:st, ˌkwɔ:təpɑ:st ('faɪv)]	Viertel nach
	quarter to [ˌkwɔ:tə 'tu:, ˌkwɔ:tətʊ ('faɪv)]	Viertel vor
	to **have breakfast** [hæv 'brekfəst]	frühstücken
3	**Saturday** ['sætədeɪ]	Samstag
◎ HV 3A	**afternoon** [ˌɑ:ftə'nu:n]	Nachmittag
	boyfriend ['bɔɪfrend]	Freund
	evening ['i:vnɪŋ]	Abend
	late [leɪt].	spät
	shop [ʃɒp]	Laden, Geschäft
	there [ðeə]	da, dort
3B	**does not, doesn't** [dʌz nɒt, 'dʌznt]	Hilfsverb für die Gegenwart (Verneinung)
	her [hɜ:]	ihr/e
	on Saturday [ɒn 'sætədeɪ]	am Samstag
	them [ðem]	sie, ihnen
3C	**do not, don't** [du: nɒt, dəʊnt]	Hilfsverb für die Gegenwart (Verneinung)
◎ HV 3D	to **speak, spoke** [spi:k, spəʊk]	sprechen
3E	to **ride a motorbike, rode** [ˌraɪd ə 'məʊtəbaɪk, rəʊd]	Motorradfahren
4A	**by bus** [baɪ 'bʌs]	mit dem Bus
	to **do, did** [du:, dɪd]	tun, machen
	doctor ['dɒktə]	Arzt / Ärztin
	Friday ['fraɪdeɪ]	Freitag
	in front of [ɪn 'frʌnt‿əv]	vor
	to **know, knew** [nəʊ, nju:]	wissen
	Monday ['mʌndeɪ]	Montag
	more [mɔ:]	mehr
	to **say, said** [seɪ, sed]	sagen
	sporty ['spɔ:tɪ]	sportlich
	stupid ['stju:pɪd]	dumm
	Sunday ['sʌndeɪ]	Sonntag
	that [ðæt]	dass
	to **walk** [wɔ:k]	gehen
	weekend [ˌwi:k'end]	Wochenende
4B	**week** [wi:k]	Woche
4C	**unsporty** [ʌn'spɔ:tɪ]	unsportlich
5A	to **live** [lɪv]	leben, wohnen
	Munich ['mju:nɪk]	München
5B	**day** [deɪ]	Tag
	Thursday ['θɜ:zdeɪ]	Donnerstag
	Tuesday ['tju:zdeɪ]	Dienstag
	Wednesday ['wenzdeɪ]	Mittwoch

Unit 3

	image ['ɪmɪdʒ]	Aussehen
	style [staɪl]	Stil
1A	**clothes** [kləʊðz]	Bekleidung
1B	**can, could** [kæn, kʊd]	können
	house [haʊs]	Haus
	interview ['ɪntəvju:]	Vorstellungsgespräch
	party ['pɑ:tɪ]	Party
	to **wear, wore** [weə]	(Kleidung) tragen
	where [weə]	wo(hin)
2	**colour** ['kʌlə]	Farbe
2A	**black** [blæk]	schwarz
	blue [blu:]	blau
	brown [braʊn]	braun
	green [gri:n]	grün
	red [red]	rot
	white [waɪt]	weiß
	yellow ['jeləʊ]	gelb
2B	**jacket** ['dʒækɪt]	Jacke
	pullover ['pʊləʊvə]	Pullover
	shirt [ʃɜ:t]	Hemd
	shoes [ʃu:z]	Schuhe
	skirt [skɜ:t]	Rock
	top [tɒp]	Oberteil, Top
	trousers ['traʊzəz]	Hose
	T-shirt ['ti:ʃɜ:t]	T-Shirt

Unit 3

2C	**Do you like ...?** [du: ju: 'laɪk, dəjə 'laɪk]	Magst du ...?/ Mögen Sie ...?/ Mögt ihr ...?
	Does it go with ...? [dʌz‿ɪt ˌgəʊ‿wɪð '...]	Passt es zu ...?
	together [tə'geðə]	zusammen
2D	**jeans** [dʒi:nz]	Jeans
3	**right** [raɪt]	richtig
◎ HV 3A	**Good luck** [ˌgʊd 'lʌk]	Viel Glück
	like that [laɪk 'ðæt]	auf diese Art und Weise
	on your way [ˌɒn jɔ: 'weɪ]	auf dem Weg
	problem ['prɒbləm]	Problem
	why [waɪ]	warum
3B	**letter** ['letə]	Brief
◎ HV 3B	**at home** [ət 'həʊm]	zu Hause
	Dear [dɪə]	Liebe/r
	next [nekst]	nächste/r/s
	nice [naɪs]	schön, nett, gut
	over ['əʊvə]	über
	to **put, put** [pʊt]	stellen, legen, setzen
	to **smoke** [sməʊk]	rauchen
	tip [tɪp]	Hinweis
	to **wash** [wɒʃ]	waschen
3C	**cigarette** ['sɪgəret]	Zigarette
	clean [kli:n]	sauber
	hair [heə]	Haar
	help [help]	Hilfe
	piercing ['pɪəsɪŋ]	Piercing
	tattoo [tæt'u:]	Tätowierung
4	**always** ['ɔ:lweɪz]	immer
	to **be, was/were** [bi:, wɒz/wɜ:]	sein
	cannot (can't), **could not** (couldn't) ['kænɒt, kɑ:nt, kʊd nɒt, 'kʊdnt]	nicht können
4A	**Don't try** [dəʊnt‿'traɪ]	Versuchen Sie nicht
	great [greɪt]	großartig
	hard [hɑ:d]	schwierig
	him [hɪm]	ihm/ihn
	his [hɪz]	sein/e
	to **make, made** [meɪk, meɪd]	machen
	make-up ['meɪkʌp]	Schminke
	month [mʌnθ]	Monat
	new [nju:]	neu
	old [əʊld]	alt
	programme ['prəʊgræm]	Sendung
	really ['rɪəlɪ]	wirklich
	so [səʊ]	sehr
	some [sʌm]	einige
	us [ʌs]	uns
	when [wen]	wann
4B	**how** [haʊ]	wie
5C	**girlfriend** ['gɜ:lfrend]	Freundin

Unit 4

1	**year** [jɪə]	Jahr
1A	**April** ['eɪprl]	April
	August ['ɔ:gəst]	August
	cloudy ['klaʊdɪ]	wolkig
	cold [kəʊld]	kalt
	December [dɪ'sembə]	Dezember
	everything ['evrɪθɪŋ]	alles
	February ['febjʊrɪ]	Februar
	foggy ['fɒgɪ]	neblig
	full [fʊl]	voll
	to **get, got** [get, gɒt]	erhalten, bekommen
	happy ['hæpɪ]	glücklich
	hayfever ['heɪˌfi:və]	Heuschnupfen
	hot [hɒt]	heiß
	in [ɪn]	in
	January ['dʒænjʊrɪ]	Januar
	July [dʒʊ'laɪ]	Juli
	June [dʒu:n]	Juni
	March [mɑ:tʃ]	März
	May [meɪ]	Mai
	much [mʌtʃ]	viel
	November [nəʊ'vembə]	November
	October [ɒk'təʊbə]	Oktober
	on holiday [ɒn 'hɒlɪdeɪ]	in Urlaub
	to **rain** [reɪn]	regnen
	September [sep'tembə]	September
	short [ʃɔ:t]	kurz
	to **snow** [snəʊ]	schneien
	sunny ['sʌnɪ]	sonnig
	windy ['wɪndɪ]	windig
1B	to **talk** [tɔ:k]	reden, sprechen
	weather ['weðə]	Wetter
2A	**angry** ['æŋgrɪ]	sauer, zornig
	bad [bæd]	schlecht
	home [həʊm]	nach Hause
	room [ru:m]	Zimmer
	was (→ to be) [wɒz]	war
	were (→ to be) [wɜ:]	warst/waren/wart
	yesterday ['jestədeɪ]	gestern
2B	to **ask** [ɑ:sk]	fragen
	to **last** [lɑ:st]	dauern
	to **use** [ju:z]	benutzen
	word [wɜ:d]	Wort
2C	**dad** [dæd]	Papa
	ill [ɪl]	krank

Unit 4

	mum [mʌm]	Mama
	tired ['taɪəd]	müde
	unhappy [ʌn'hæpɪ]	unglücklich
2D	**laptop** ['læptɒp]	Laptop
	to **listen** ['lɪsn]	zuhören
	to **look at** ['lʊk æt, 'lʊk‿ət]	ansehen
	to **open** ['əʊpn]	öffnen
◉ HV 3A, B	to **phone** [fəʊn]	anrufen
	said (→ to say) [sed]	sagte
	to **shout** [ʃaʊt]	schreien
3B	**did** [dɪd]	Hilfsverb für die Vergangenheitsform
	did not (didn't) [dɪd nɒt, 'dɪdnt]	Hilfsverb für die Vergangenheitsform (Verneinung)
3D	to **look after** [lʊk 'ɑ:ftə]	sich kümmern um
◉ HV 3D	**best** [best]	beste/r/s
	to **buy, bought** [baɪ, bɔ:t]	kaufen
	to **check** [tʃek]	prüfen
	hard work [ˌhɑ:d 'wɜ:k]	harte Arbeit
	Spain [speɪn]	Spanien
4A	**then** [ðen]	dann
	came (→ to come) [keɪm]	kam/en
	class [klɑ:s]	Klasse
	happy pill ['hæpɪ ˌpɪl]	eine Drogenart
	to **kiss** [kɪs]	küssen
	knew (→ to know) [nju:]	kannte, wusste
	to **pay** [peɪ]	(be)zahlen
	saw (→ to see) [sɔ:]	sah/en
	today [tə'deɪ]	heute
	took (→ to take) [tʊk]	nahm/en
	was not (wasn't) [wɒz nɒt, 'wɒznt]	war nicht
	went (→ to go) [went]	ging/en
	wrong [rɒŋ]	falsch
5B	**mobile (phone)** ['məʊbaɪl]	Handy

Unit 5

	media ['mi:dɪə]	Medien
1A	**answer** ['ɑ:nsə]	Antwort
	century ['sentʃərɪ]	Jahrhundert
	to **chat** [tʃæt]	chatten
	to **give, gave** [gɪv, geɪv]	geben
	to **love** [lʌv]	lieben
1B	**other** ['ʌðə]	andere/r/s
	person ['pɜ:sn]	Person
	point [pɔɪnt]	Punkt
	thing [θɪŋ]	Ding
	to **wake up, woke up** [weɪk 'ʌp, wəʊk 'ʌp]	aufwachen
2A	**back** [bæk]	zurück
	to **borrow** ['bɒrəʊ]	leihen, ausleihen
	bye [baɪ]	Tschüss
	must, had to [mʌst]	müssen
	to **want to** ['wɒnt‿tu:, 'wɒnt‿tə]	wollen
2B	**euro** ['jʊərəʊ]	Euro
	minute ['mɪnɪt]	Minute
	to **send, sent** [send, sent]	senden, verschicken
	to **write, wrote** [raɪt, rəʊt]	schreiben
2C	**DVD player** [ˌdi:vi:'di: ˌpleɪə]	DVD Spieler
	project ['prɒdʒekt]	Projekt
2D	**blog** [blɒg]	Online-Tagebuch
	to **download** [ˌdaʊn'ləʊd]	herunterladen
	website ['websaɪt]	Website
3A	**please** [pli:z]	bitte
	See you! ['si: ˌju:]	Bis dann!
	to **text** [tekst]	eine SMS schicken
	thanks [θæŋks]	danke
	tomorrow [tə'mɒrəʊ]	morgen
◉ HV 3A	**again** [ə'geɪn, ə'gen]	wieder
	better ['betə]	besser
	to **come, came** [kʌm, keɪm]	kommen
	film [fɪlm]	Film
	hope [həʊp]	Hoffnung
	I'm sorry. [aɪm 'sɒrɪ]	Es tut mir leid.
	more important [mɔ:r‿ɪm'pɔ:tnt]	wichtiger
	quick [kwɪk]	schnell
	supermarket ['su:pəˌmɑ:kɪt]	Supermarkt
	text [tekst]	SMS
	than [ðæn]	als
	thought (→ to think) [θɔ:t]	dachte/n
	trip [trɪp]	Reise
	to **wait** [weɪt]	warten
	What kind of ...? [wɒt 'kaɪnd əv]	Was für ...?
3B	**radio** ['reɪdɪəʊ]	Radio
	song [sɒŋ]	Lied, Song
◉ HV 3B	**another** [ə'nʌðə]	noch ein/e
	different ['dɪfərnt]	etwas anderes
	name [neɪm]	Name
	on [ɒn]	eingeschaltet
4A	**after all** [ˌɑ:ftər‿'ɔ:l]	doch noch
	all over the world [ɔ:l ˌəʊvə ðə 'wɜ:ld]	auf der ganzen Welt
	any more [ˌenɪ 'mɔ:]	nicht mehr
	to **become, became** [bɪ'kʌm, bɪ'keɪm]	werden
	big [bɪg]	groß
	to **decide to** [dɪ'saɪd‿tu:, dɪ'saɪd‿tə]	entscheiden

Unit 5

	difference ['dɪfrns]	Unterschied
	first [fɜ:st]	erste/r/s
	group [gru:p]	Gruppe
	had (→ to have) [hæd]	hatte(n)
	to **know each other, knew each other** ['nəʊ‿i:tʃˌʌðə, 'nju:‿i:tʃˌʌðə]	sich kennen
	most famous [məʊst 'feɪməs]	der / die / das berühmteste
	of course [əv 'kɔ:s]	natürlich
	rumour ['ru:mə]	Gerücht
	to **sing, sang** [sɪŋ, sæŋ]	singen
	solo career [ˌsəʊləʊ kə'rɪə]	Solokarriere
	to **start** [stɑ:t]	anfangen
	to **stay** [steɪ]	bleiben
4B	**before** [bɪ'fɔ:]	vor, bevor
5A	**DVD shop** [ˌdi:vi:'di: ˌʃɒp]	DVD-Verleih

Unit 6

	a place to live [ə ˌpleɪs tʊ 'lɪv]	ein Wohnort
1A	**bridge** [brɪdʒ]	Brücke
	church [tʃɜ:tʃ]	Kirche
	country ['kʌntrɪ]	Land
	factory ['fæktrɪ]	Fabrik
	farm [fɑ:m]	Bauernhof
	field [fi:ld]	Feld
	park [pɑ:k]	Park
	river ['rɪvə]	Fluss
	road [rəʊd]	Straße
	station ['steɪʃn]	Bahnhof
	town [taʊn]	Stadt
	village ['vɪlɪdʒ]	Dorf
	wood [wʊd]	Wald
2	**bored** [bɔ:d]	gelangweilt
2A	to **phone** [fəʊn]	telefonieren
	to **read, read** [ri:d, red]	lesen
	to **work** [wɜ:k]	arbeiten
2B	**at the moment** [ət‿ðə 'məʊmənt]	im Moment
2C	**flat** [flæt]	Wohnung
	It sounds great! [ɪt‿saʊndz 'greɪt]	Das klingt gut!
	near [nɪə]	in der Nähe von
	to **tell, told** [tel, təʊld]	erzählen
◉ HV 3A	**lucky** ['lʌkɪ]	Glück haben
	part [pɑ:t]	Teil
	probably ['prɒbəblɪ]	wahrscheinlich
	stadium ['steɪdɪəm]	Stadion
	swimming pool ['swɪmɪŋ ˌpu:l]	Hallenbad
	What about ...? [ˌwɒt‿ə'baʊt]	Was ist mit ...?
3B	**bed** [bed]	Bett
◉ HV 3B, C	to **bring, brought** [brɪŋ, brɔ:t]	bringen
	money ['mʌnɪ]	Geld
	plan [plæn]	Plan
4A	**all** [ɔ:l]	alle
	article ['ɑ:tɪkl]	Artikel
	to **cook** [kʊk]	kochen
	drug [drʌg]	Droge
	drunken ['drʌŋkn]	betrunken
	to **eat, ate** [i:t, eɪt / et]	essen
	exciting [ɪk'saɪtɪŋ]	spannend, aufregend
	healthy ['helθɪ]	gesund
	nothing ['nʌθɪŋ]	nichts
	people ['pi:pl]	Leute
	to **ring, rang** [rɪŋ, ræŋ]	klingeln
	to **sell, sold** [sel, səʊld]	verkaufen
	to **steal, stole** [sti:l, stəʊl]	stehlen
	this evening [ðɪs 'i:vnɪŋ]	heute Abend
	train [treɪn]	Zug
	who [hu:]	wer
	worried ['wʌrɪd]	besorgt
	to **worry** ['wʌrɪ]	sich Sorgen machen
5A	**hospital** ['hɒspɪtl]	Krankenhaus
	policewoman [pə'li:sˌwʊman]	Polizistin
	tourist ['tʊərɪst]	Tourist/in
	youth club ['ju:θ ˌklʌb]	Jugendtreff

Unit 7

	culture ['kʌltʃə]	Kultur
1A	**beef stroganoff** [ˌbi:f 'strɒgənɒf]	Rind à la Stroganoff
	fish and chips [ˌfɪʃn'tʃɪps]	Fisch mit Pommes Frites
	food [fu:d]	Essen, Lebensmittel
	Italy ['ɪtəlɪ]	Italien
	Russia ['rʌʃə]	Russland
	the USA [ðə ˌju:es'eɪ]	die Vereinigten Staaten
	Turkey ['tɜ:kɪ]	Türkei
1C	**Italian** [ɪ'tælɪən]	italienisch
	language ['læŋgwɪdʒ]	Sprache
	Russian ['rʌʃən]	russisch
	Spanish ['spænɪʃ]	spanisch
	Turkish ['tɜ:kɪʃ]	türkisch
2A	**extra** ['ekstrə]	zusätzlich
	lesson ['lesn]	Stunde
	to **organise** ['ɔ:gənaɪz]	organisieren
	student ['stju:dənt]	Schüler/in

Unit 7

	to **understand, understood** [ˌʌndə'stænd, ˌʌndə'stʊd]	verstehen
2B	**hungry** ['hʌŋgrɪ]	hungrig
	enough [ɪ'nʌf]	genug
	to **find, found** [faɪnd, faʊnd]	finden
	to **lend, lent** [lend, lent]	leihen
2D	**idea** [aɪ'dɪə]	Idee
3A	**Bonfire Night** ['bɒnfaɪə ˌnaɪt]	der 5. November (Großbritannien)
	St Patrick's Day [ʃənt‿'pætrɪks ˌdeɪ]	irischer Nationalfeiertag am 17. März
HV3A	**as** [æz, əz]	wie
	barbecue ['bɑ:bɪkju:]	Grillfest
	to **celebrate** ['seləbreɪt]	feiern
	to **dress up** [dres 'ʌp]	sich verkleiden
	every ['evrɪ]	jede/r/s
	fire [faɪə]	Feuer
	firework ['faɪəwɜ:k]	Feuerwerk
	ghost [gəʊst]	Geist
	Ireland ['aɪələnd]	Irland
	outside [ˌaʊt'saɪd]	draußen
	parade [pə'reɪd]	Umzug
	sweet [swi:t]	Süßigkeit
	trick or treat [ˌtrɪkɔ:'tri:t]	Spruch, den Kinder an Halloween aufsagen
	usually ['ju:ʒəlɪ]	normalerweise
	witch [wɪtʃ]	Hexe
3D	**Australia** [ɒs'treɪlɪə]	Australien
	Canada ['kænədə]	Kanada
	New Zealand [ˌnju:'zi:lənd]	Neuseeland
	Scotland ['skɒtlənd]	Schottland
	Thanksgiving [ˌθæŋks'gɪvɪŋ, 'θæŋksˌgɪvɪŋ]	Erntedankfest in den Vereinigten Staaten
◎HV3D	**city** ['sɪtɪ]	Stadt
	crocodile ['krɒkədaɪl]	Krokodil
	grandparents ['grænˌpeərnts]	Großeltern
	kangaroo ['kæŋgəru:]	Känguru
	koala [kəʊ'ɑ:lə]	Koalabär
	like [laɪk]	wie
	sheep [ʃi:p]	Schaf
	to **surf** [sɜ:f]	surfen
	well [wel]	nun, also
4A	**Africa** ['æfrɪkə]	Afrika
	all over [ɔ:l 'əʊvə]	überall
	Britain ['brɪtn]	Großbritannien
	capital ['kæpɪtl]	Hauptstadt
	European [ˌjʊərə'pɪən]	europäisch
	independent [ˌɪndɪ'pendnt]	unabhängig
	India ['ɪndɪə]	Indien
	multi-cultural [ˌmʌltɪ'kʌltʃərəl]	multikulturell
	nationality [ˌnæʃə'nælətɪ]	Nationalität
	non-white [ˌnɒn'waɪt]	nicht Weiße/r
	North America [ˌnɔ:θə'merɪkə]	Nordamerika
	Olympic Games [əˌlɪmpɪk‿'geɪmz]	die Olympischen Spiele
	once [wʌns, wɒns]	einmal
	side [saɪd]	Seite
	world [wɜ:ld]	Welt
4C	**next to** ['nekst tu:]	neben
6B	**door** [dɔ:]	Tür
	I will / I'll [aɪ wɪl, aɪl]	ich werde

Activity page 1

a few [ə 'fju:]	ein paar
back [bæk]	Rückseite
basketball ['bɑ:skɪtbɔ:l]	Basketball
card [kɑ:d]	Karte
to **cut out, cut out** [kʌt 'aʊt, kʌt 'aʊt]	ausschneiden

Activity page 2

dead [ded]	tot
to **finish** ['fɪnɪʃ]	fertig sein
floor [flɔ:]	Fußboden
garden ['gɑ:dn]	Garten
killer ['kɪlə]	Mörder/in
last [lɑ:st]	letzte/r
light [laɪt]	Licht
police [pə'li:s]	Polizei
post office ['pəʊst ˌɒfɪs]	Postamt
to **turn around** [tɜ:n ə'raʊnd]	umdrehen
was killed [wɒz 'kɪld, wəz 'kɪld]	wurde umgebracht

Alphabetische Wortliste

A

a	ein/e	1/2C
a few	ein paar	AP/1
a place to live	ein Wohnort	6/1
about	über	1/1
Africa	Afrika	7/4A
after all	doch noch	5/4A
afternoon	Nachmittag	2/HV 3A
again	wieder	5/HV 3A
all	alle	6/4A
all over	überall	7/4A
all over the world	auf der ganzen Welt	5/4A
always	immer	3/4
and	und	1/1
angry	sauer, zornig	4/2A
another	noch ein/e	5/HV 3B
answer	Antwort	5/1A
any more	nicht mehr	5/4A
April	April	4/1A
to **arrive**	ankommen	2/2C
article	Artikel	6/4A
as	wie	7/HV 3A
to **ask**	fragen	4/2B
at	an	1/3B
at home	zu Hause	3/HV 3B
at six o'clock	um sechs Uhr	2/1A
at the moment	im Moment	6/2B
August	August	4/1A
Australia	Australien	7/3D

B

back	Rückseite	AP/1
back	zurück	5/2A
bad	schlecht	4/2A
barbecue	Grillfest	7/HV 3A
basketball	Basketball	AP/1
to **be, was/were**	sein	3/4
because	weil	2/2A
to **become, became**	werden	5/4A
bed	Bett	6/3B
beef stroganoff	Rind à la Stroganoff	7/1A
before	vor, bevor	5/4B
best	beste/r	4/HV 3D
Best wishes.	Alles Gute.	1/4A
better	besser	5/HV 3A
big	groß	5/4A
black	schwarz	3/2A
blog	Online-Tagebuch	5/2D
blue	blau	3/2A
Bonfire Night	der 5. November (Großbritannien)	7/3A
book	Buch	1/3D
bored	gelangweilt	6/2
to **borrow**	leihen, ausleihen	5/2A
boy	Junge	1/1A
boyfriend	Freund	2/HV 3A
bridge	Brücke	6/1A
to **bring, brought**	bringen	6/HV 3B, C
Britain	Großbritannien	7/4A
brother	Bruder	1/2
brown	braun	3/2A
but	aber	1/4A
to **buy, bought**	kaufen	4/HV 3D
by bus	mit dem Bus	2/4A
bye	Tschüss	5/2A

C

came (→ to come)	kam/en	4/4A
can, could	können	3/1B
Canada	Kanada	7/3D
cannot (can't), **could not** (couldn't)	nicht können	3/4
capital	Hauptstadt	7/4A
car	Auto	2/1A
card	Karte	AP/1
cat	Katze	1/4A
CD	CD	1/3A
to **celebrate**	feiern	7/HV 3A
century	Jahrhundert	5/1A
to **chat**	chatten	5/1A
to **check**	prüfen	4/HV 3D
church	Kirche	6/1A
cigarette	Zigarette	3/3C
cinema	Kino	2/1A
city	Stadt	7/HV 3D
class	Klasse	4/4A
clean	sauber	3/3C
clothes	Bekleidung	3/1A
cloudy	wolkig	4/1A
cold	kalt	4/1A
college	Berufs(fach)schule	1/4A
colour	Farbe	3/2
to **come, came**	kommen	5/HV 3A
computer	Computer	2/1A
to **cook**	kochen	6/4A
cool	cool	1/1
country	Land	6/1A
crocodile	Krokodil	7/HV 3D
culture	Kultur	7/1
to **cut out, cut out**	ausschneiden	AP/1

D

dad	Papa	4/2C
day	Tag	2/5B
dead	tot	AP/2
Dear	Liebe/r	3/HV 3B
December	Dezember	4/1A
to **decide to**	entscheiden	5/4A
did	Hilfsverb für die Vergangenheitsform	4/3B
did not (didn't)	Hilfsverb für die Vergangenheitsform (Verneinung)	4/3B
difference	Unterschied	5/4A
different	etwas anderes	5/HV 3B
disco	Disko	1/1C
do not, don't	Hilfsverb für die Gegenwart (Verneinung)	2/3C
Do you like?	Magst du?/Mögen Sie?/Mögt ihr?	3/2C
to **do, did**	tun, machen	2/4A
doctor	Arzt/Ärztin	2/4A
Does it go with…?	Passt es zu …?	3/2C
does not, doesn't	Hilfsverb für die Gegenwart (Verneinung)	2/3B
Don't try	Versuchen Sie nicht	3/4A
door	Tür	7/6B
to **download**	herunterladen	5/2D
to **dress up**	sich verkleiden	7/HV 3A
to **drive, drove**	fahren	2/1A
drug	Droge	6/4A
drunken	betrunken	6/4A
DVD player	DVD Spieler	5/2C
DVD shop	DVD-Verleih	5/5A

E

to **eat, ate**	essen	6/4A
email	E-Mail	1/4
England	England	1/1
English	Engländer/in	1/1
enough	genug	7/2B
euro	Euro	5/2B
European	europäisch	7/4A
evening	Abend	2/HV 3A
every	jede/r/s	7/HV 3A
everything	alles	4/1A
exciting	spannend, aufregend	6/4A
extra	zusätzlich	7/2A

F

factory	Fabrik	6/1A
family, families	Familie	1/3
fan	Fan	1/4A
farm	Bauernhof	6/1A
father	Vater	1/4A
favourite	Lieblings-	1/4A
February	Februar	4/1A
field	Feld	6/1A
film	Film	5/HV 3A
to **find, found**	finden	7/2B
to **finish**	fertig sein	AP/2
fire	Feuer	7/HV 3A
firework	Feuerwerk	7/HV 3A
first	erste/r/s	5/4A
fish and chips	Fisch mit Pommes Frites	7/1A
flat	Wohnung	6/2C
floor	Fußboden	AP/2
foggy	neblig	4/1A
food	Essen, Lebensmittel	7/1A
football	Fußball	1/4A
for	für	2/2A
free time	Freizeit	2/1
Friday	Freitag	2/4A
friend	Freund/in	1/4A
friendly	nett, freundlich	1/4A
from	aus, von	1/1
full	voll	4/1A
fun	Spaß	1/4A

G

game	Spiel	2/2A
garden	Garten	AP/2
German	deutsch	1/4A
Germany	Deutschland	1/5A
to **get up, got up**	aufstehen	2/1A
to **get, got**	erhalten, bekommen	4/1A
ghost	Geist	7/HV 3A
girl	Mädchen	1/1A
girlfriend	Freundin	3/5C
to **give, gave**	geben	5/1A
to **go, went**	gehen, fahren	2/1A
good	gut	1/4A
Good luck.	Viel Glück.	3/HV 3A
grandparents	Großeltern	7/HV 3D
great	großartig	3/4A
green	grün	3/2A
group	Gruppe	5/4A

H

had (→ to have)	hatte/n	5/4A
hair	Haar	3/3C
half past	halb	2/2C
happy	glücklich	4/1A
happy pill	eine Drogenart	4/4A
hard	schwierig, hart	3/4A
hard work	harte Arbeit	4/HV 3D
has got	hat	1/3E
to **have breakfast**	frühstücken	2/2C
to **have got**	haben	1/3B
hayfever	Heuschnupfen	4/1A
he is (he's)	er ist	1/1A
healthy	gesund	6/4A
help	Hilfe	3/3C
her	ihr/e	2/3B
here	hier	1/2
hi	Hi	1/2B
him	ihm	3/4A
his	sein/e	3/4A
home	nach Hause	4/2A
hope	Hoffnung	5/HV 3A
hospital	Krankenhaus	6/5A
hot	heiß	4/1A
house	Haus	3/1B
how	wie	3/4B
hungry	hungrig	7/2B

I

I am (I'm)	ich bin	1/1
I will (I'll)	ich werde	7/6B
I'm sorry.	Es tut mir leid.	5/HV 3A
I've got	ich habe	1/HV 3A
idea	Idee	7/2D
ill	krank	4/2C
image	Aussehen	3/1
in	in	4/1A
in front of	vor	2/4A
in the photo	auf dem Foto	1/1A
independent	unabhängig	7/4A
India	Indien	7/4A
interview	Vorstellungs-gespräch	3/1B
Ireland	Irland	7/HV 3A
is	ist	1/1A
it	es	1/4A
It sounds great!	Das klingt gut!	6/2C
Italian	italienisch	7/1C
Italy	Italien	7/1A

J

jacket	Jacke	3/2B
January	Januar	4/1A
jeans	Jeans	3/2D
job	Job	1/4A
July	Juli	4/1A
June	Juni	4/1A

K

kangaroo	Känguru	7/HV 3D
killer	Mörder/in	AP/2
to **kiss**	küssen	4/4A
knew (→ to know)	kannte, wusste	4/4A
to **know each other, knew each other**	sich kennen	5/4A
to **know, knew**	wissen	2/4A
koala	Koalabär	7/HV 3D

L

language	Sprache	7/1C
laptop	Laptop	4/2D
to **last**	dauern	4/2B
last	letzte/r	AP/2
late	spät	2/HV 3A
to **leave, left**	verlassen	2/2C
to **lend, lent**	leihen	7/2B
lesson	Stunde	7/2A
letter	Brief	3/3B
light	Licht	AP/2
to **like**	mögen	2/2A
like	wie	7/HV 3D
like that	auf diese Art und Weise	3/HV 3A
to **listen**	zuhören	4/2D
to **live**	leben, wohnen	2/5A
to **look**	schauen	1/HV 3D
to **look after**	sich kümmern um	4/3D
to **look at**	ansehen	4/2D
lots of	viel/e	1/4A
to **love**	lieben	5/1A
lucky	Glück haben	6/HV HV 3A

M

magazine	Zeitschrift	2/2A
to **make, made**	machen	3/4A
make-up	Schminke	3/4A
March	März	4/1A
May	Mai	4/1A
me	mich, mir	1/1
media	Medien	5/1
to **meet, met**	(sich) treffen (mit)	2/1A
minute	Minute	6/2B
mobile (phone)	Handy	4/5B
Monday	Montag	2/4A

money	Geld	6 / HV 3B, C
month	Monat	3 / 4A
more	mehr	2 / 4A
more important	wichtiger	5 / HV 3A
morning	Morgen	2 / 2C
most famous	der / die / das berühmteste	5 / 4A
mother	Mutter	1 / 4A
motorbike	Motorrad	2 / 2A
Mr	Herr	1 / 4A
Mrs	Frau (bei verheirateten Frauen)	1 / 4A
much	viel	4 / 1A
multi-cultural	multikulturell	7 / 4A
mum	Mama	4 / 2C
Munich	München	2 / 5A
music	Musik	1 / 1C
must, had to	müssen	5 / 2A
my	mein/e	1 / 2

N

name	Name	5 / HV 3B
nationality	Nationalität	7 / 4A
near	in der Nähe von	6 / 2C
never	nie(mals)	2 / 1A
new	neu	3 / 4A
New Zealand	Neuseeland	7 / 3D
next	nächste/r/s	3 / HV 3B
next to	neben	7 / 4C
nice	schön, nett, gut	3 / HV 3B
no	nein; kein	1 / 4A
non-white	nicht Weiße/r	7 / 4A
North America	Nordamerika	7 / 4A
not	nicht	1 / 2B
nothing	nichts	6 / 4A
November	November	4 / 1A
now	jetzt	1 / 2C
number	Zahl, Nummer	1 / 5B

O

October	Oktober	4 / 1A
of	von, bei, aus	1 / 4A
of course	natürlich	5 / 4A
often	oft	2 / 1A
old	alt	3 / 4A
Olympic Games	die Olympischen Spiele	7 / 4A
on	eingeschaltet	5 / HV 3B
on holiday	in Urlaub	4 / 1A
on Saturday	am Samstag	2 / 3B
on your way	auf dem Weg	3 / HV 3A
once	einmal	7 / 4A
one	ein/e	1 / HV3A
to **open**	öffnen	4 / 2D
or	oder	1 / 4B
to **organise**	organisieren	7 / 2A
other	andere/r/s	5 / 1B
our	unser	1 / 4A
outside	draußen	7 / HV 3A
over	über	3 / HV 3B

P

parade	Umzug	7 / HV 3A
parents	Eltern	1 / 4A
park	Park	6 / 1A
part	Teil	6 / HV 3A
partner	Partner/in	1 / 3D
party	Party	3 / 1B
to **pay**	(be)zahlen	4 / 4A
people	Leute	6 / 4A
person	Person	5 / 1B
to **phone**	anrufen	4 / HV 3A, B
to **phone**	telefonieren	6 / 2A
piercing	Piercing	3 / 3C
plan	Plan	6 / HV 3B, C
to **play**	spielen; Sport machen	2 / 1A
please	bitte	5 / 3A
point	Punkt	5 / 1B
police	Polizei	AP / 2
policewoman	Polizistin	5 / 5A
post office	Postamt	AP / 2
probably	wahrscheinlich	6 / HV 3A
problem	Problem	3 / HV 3A
programme	Sendung	3 / 4A
project	Projekt	5 / 2C
pullover	Pullover	3 / 2B
to **put, put**	stellen, legen, setzen	3 / HV 3B

Q

quarter past	Viertel nach	2 / 2C
quarter to	Viertel vor	2 / 2C
question	Frage	1 / 5D
quick	schnell	5 / HV 3A

R

Rachel's	Rachels	1 / 4B
radio	Radio	5 / 3B
to **rain**	regnen	4 / 1A
to **read, read**	lesen	6 / 2A
really	wirklich	3 / 4A

red	rot	3/2A
to **ride a motorbike, rode**	Motorradfahren	2/3E
right	richtig	3/3
to **ring, rang**	klingeln	6/4A
river	Fluss	6/1A
road	Straße	6/1A
room	Zimmer	4/2A
rumour	Gerücht	5/4A
Russia	Russland	7/1A
Russian	russisch	7/1C

S

said (→ to say)	sagte	4/HV 3A, B
Saturday	Samstag	2/3
saw (→ to see)	sah/en	4/4A
to **say, said**	sagen	2/4A
Scotland	Schottland	7/3D
See you!	Bis dann!	5/3A
to **sell, sold**	verkaufen	6/4A
to **send, sent**	senden, verschicken	5/2B
September	September	4/1A
she is (she's)	sie ist	1/1A
sheep	Schaf	7/HV 3D
shirt	Hemd	3/2B
shoes	Schuhe	3/2B
shop	Laden, Geschäft	2/HV 3A
shopping	Einkaufen	2/2A
short	kurz	4/1A
to **shout**	schreien	4/HV 3A, B
side	Seite	7/4A
to **sing, sang**	singen	5/4A
sister	Schwester	1/2
to **sit, sat**	sitzen	2/1A
skirt	Rock	3/2B
to **smoke**	rauchen	3/HV 3B
to **snow**	schneien	4/1A
so	sehr	3/4A
solo career	Solokarriere	5/4A
some	einige	3/4A
sometimes	manchmal	2/1A
song	Lied, Song	5/3B
Spain	Spanien	4/HV 3D
Spanish	spanisch	7/1C
to **speak, spoke**	sprechen	2/HV 3D
sport	Sport	2/1A
sporty	sportlich	2/4A
St Patrick's Day	irischer Nationalfeiertag am 17. März	7/3A
stadium	Stadion	6/HV 3A
to **start**	anfangen	5/4A
station	Bahnhof	6/1A
to **stay**	bleiben	5/4A
to **steal, stole**	stehlen	6/4A
student	Schüler/in	7/2A
stupid	dumm	2/4A
style	Stil	3/1
Sunday	Sonntag	2/4A
sunny	sonnig	4/1A
supermarket	Supermarkt	5/HV 3A
to **surf**	surfen	7/HV 3D
sweet	Süßigkeit	7/HV 3A
swimming pool	Hallenbad	6/HV 3A

T

to **talk**	reden, sprechen	4/1B
tattoo	Tätowierung	3/3C
teacher	Lehrer/in	1/4A
team	Team, Mannschaft	1/4A
teenager	Teenager	2/1
to **tell, told**	erzählen	6/2C
to **text**	eine SMS schicken	5/3A
text	SMS	5/HV 3A
than	als	5/HV 3A
thanks	danke	5/3A
Thanksgiving	Erntedankfest in den Vereinigten Staaten	7/3D
that	dass	2/4A
that's	das ist	1/4A
the	der/die/das	1/1A
the USA	die Vereinigten Staaten	7/1A
their	ihr/e	2/1A
them	sie, ihnen	2/3B
then	dann	4/4A
there	da, dort	2/HV 3A
there are	es gibt	1/4A
there's	es gibt	1/4A
they are (they're)	sie sind	1/2
thing	Ding	5/1B
to **think, thought**	denken, meinen	2/2A
this	diese/r/s	1/4A
this evening	heute Abend	6/4A
thought (→ to think)	dachte/n	5/HV 3A
Thursday	Donnerstag	2/5B
tip	Hinweis	3/HV 3B
tired	müde	4/2C
to	zu	2/1A
today	heute	4/4A
together	zusammen	3/2C
tomorrow	morgen	5/3A

too	auch, zu	1/1
took (→ to take)	nahm/en	4/4A
top	Oberteil, Top	3/2B
tourist	Tourist/in	5/5A
town	Stadt	6/1A
train	Zug	6/4A
trick or treat	Spruch, der Kinder an Halloween aufsagen	7/HV 3A
trip	Reise	5/HV 3A
trousers	Hose	3/2B
T-shirt	T-Shirt	3/2B
Tuesday	Dienstag	2/5B
Turkey	Türkei	7/1A
Turkish	türkisch	7/1C
to **turn around**	umdrehen	AP/2
TV soap	Seifenoper im Fernsehen	2/2A
two	zwei	1/HV 3A

U

to **understand, understood**	verstehen	7/2A
unhappy	unglücklich	4/2C
unsporty	unsportlich	2/4C
us	uns	3/4A
to **use**	benutzen	4/2B
usually	normalerweise	7/HV 3A

V

very	sehr	1/4A
village	Dorf	6/1A
to **visit**	besuchen	2/1A

W

to **wait**	warten	5/HV 3A
to **wake up, woke up**	aufwachen	5/1B
to **walk**	gehen	2/4A
walking	Wandern, Spazierengehen	2/2A
to **want to**	wollen	5/2A
was (→ to be)	war	4/2A
was killed	wurde umgebracht	AP/2
was not (wasn't)	war nicht	4/4A
to **wash**	waschen	3/HV 3B
to **watch TV**	fernsehen	2/1A
we are (we're)	wir sind	1/4A
to **wear, wore**	tragen (Kleidung)	3/1B
weather	Wetter	4/1B
website	Website	5/2D
Wednesday	Mittwoch	2/5B
week	Woche	2/4B
weekend	Wochenende	2/4A
well	nun, also	7/HV 3D
went (→ to go)	ging/en	4/4A
were (→ to be)	warst/waren/wart	4/2A
What about...?	Was ist mit ...?	6/HV 3A
What have I got?	Was habe ich?	1/HV 3D
What kind of ...?	Was für ...?	5/HV 3A
What's?	Was ist?	1/1D
when	wann	3/4A
where	wo(hin)	3/1B
white	weiß	3/2A
who	wer	6/4A
Who's?	Wer ist?	2/2A
why	warum	3/HV 3A
windy	windig	4/1A
witch	Hexe	7/HV 3A
with	mit	1/4A
wood	Wald	6/1A
word	Wort	4/2B
to **work**	arbeiten	6/2A
world	Welt	7/4A
worried	besorgt	6/4A
to **worry**	sich Sorgen machen	6/4A
to **write, wrote**	schreiben	5/2B
wrong	falsch	4/4A

Y

year	Jahr	4/1
yellow	gelb	3/2A
yes	ja	1/2B
yesterday	gestern	4/2A
you are (you're)	du bist/Sie sind/ihr seid	1/2B
your	dein/Ihr/euer	1/3C
youth club	Jugendtreff	6/5A

Hörverstehenstexte

Die hier nicht aufgeführten Texte der Lehrer-Audio-CD sind bereits im vorderen Teil des Buches in den Units abgedruckt.

Unit 1 Listening, 3A

1. I'm Maggie. And I've got two sisters.
2. I'm Leo. I've got a brother. He's cool.
3. And I'm Joe. I've got a sister. Yes, one little sister.
4. Hi, I'm Paula. I've got two brothers. Yuck!

Unit 1 Listening, 3D

I'm Dot. I haven't got a partner.
What have I got? I haven't got a brother.
I've got a book – look! But I've got a sister.
I've got a CD – gee! I've just kissed her!

Unit 2 Listening, Anna's Saturday, 3A

I get up late on Saturday morning.
I have breakfast.
Then I go to the shops.
I meet my friends at MacBurger.
We have a hamburger there.
Then I go home.
I sit at my computer in the afternoon.
In the evening I meet my boyfriend Paul.
We have a good time.

Unit 2 Listening, 3D, 3E

Anna's brother likes music.
He doesn't speak German.
He likes magazines.
He doesn't watch TV.
He rides a motorbike.
He doesn't play football.

Unit 3 Listening, The right clothes? 3A

John is in town. He meets Pat.

Pat Hi, John.
John Hello, Pat.
Pat Why aren't you at college?
John I've got a job interview. And you?
Pat I'm going to the doctor's. And you've got an interview?
John Yes. At 10 o'clock. At Smith's Garage.
Pat And you're on your way there now?
John Yes, I am.
Pat And you're going to the interview like that?
John Yes. What's the problem?
Pat No problem. Er, good luck!

Unit 3 Listening, The right clothes? 3B

John is with his mother. He has got a letter.

John Mum, I've got a letter from Smith's Garage, the job interview. … Oh no!
Mum What's the problem?
John Listen!
"Dear Mr Watson,
You haven't got the job.
Here are some tips for your next interview:
Leave your piercing at home.
Put a shirt over your tattoo.
Wear clean shoes.
Wear clean trousers.
Wear a nice jacket, not a jeans jacket.
Wash your hair.
Don't smoke cigarettes at the interview.
Don't wear a disco shirt."

Unit 4 Listening, Sam's problems, 3A, B

Richard is with Sam.

Sam My day wasn't very good.
Richard What was the problem?
Sam My girlfriend Joanne was angry with me.
She phoned me.

She shouted at me.
She asked me lots of questions.
She said I was stupid.
She used bad words.
She didn't listen to me.

Unit 4 Listening, Sam's problems, 3C

Richard is still talking to Sam.

Richard What did you do?
Sam My girlfriend was in Spain with her best friend. She asked me to do lots of things for her.
But …
I didn't look after her cat.
I didn't check her motorbike.
I didn't help her dad.
I didn't buy her chocolates.
I didn't phone her on holiday.
And I didn't meet her at the airport!!
Richard That isn't a problem. That girlfriend is hard work!

Unit 5 Listening, Time for texting, 3A

a) **Paul** Where were you yesterday?
Lisa I'm sorry.
Paul I waited and waited for you, but you didn't come.
Lisa I said I was sorry. I was at home. My mother was ill.
Paul So your mother is more important than me? I thought you loved me. Bye, Sue. See you at college.

b) **Sue** That film was really bad.
Carol Yes. Car Wars 3 was much better.
Sue Where's Daniel today, Carol?
Carol He's at home. Oh no!
Sue What's the problem?
Carol He wanted to see Car Wars 4 with his friend Tim.
I must send him a text. I hope he's OK now. He was ill yesterday.

c) **Ben** I don't know what kind of pizza Lucy likes.
Harry Then send her a text.
Ben OK. Now what pizzas have they got in this supermarket?
Harry Be quick. I'm hungry!

d) **Mechanic** Your car is OK again now.
John Thanks very much.
Mechanic Where are you going?
John London.
Mechanic OK. Have a good trip.
John Thanks. Bye. OK, now before I leave I must send a text to Jill.

Unit 5 Listening, 3B

Now Carol and Sue are at Sue's house.

Sue Oh! My radio is on.
Carol Oh no. That's Soft Radio. They only play old songs.
Sue Yes, but some of the old songs are really good.
Carol My parents listen to lots of old songs and I don't often like them.
Radio Here's Elton John with an old favourite, Daniel.
Carol Daniel? That's different. That's a great song!
Sue And I know why. Your boyfriend's name is Daniel!
Carol OK, OK. Now listen, and then we can go online and download the song. And then I must send Daniel a text.
Sue Another text?? You and Daniel!

Unit 6 Listening, In the town, 3A

Pat is still talking to her friend Debbie.

Pat So what other places are near your flat?
Debbie There's a big football stadium, Arsenal.
Pat What about a swimming pool?
Debbie I have to get the bus to the swimming pool.

	It's about 2 miles from here. It's near my college.
Pat	You said there were lots of shops. Is there a supermarket near you?
Debbie	Yes, there is. It's only two minutes from here.
Pat	Right! But you probably live near a big factory.
Debbie	No, I don't. There are no factories near here. This is a really nice part of town. There's a big park too.
Pat	You're so lucky, Debbie.
Debbie	Look, why don't you come and visit me here in London next month? Then you can see how nice it is here.
Pat	Thanks, Debbie. That's a great idea.

Unit 6 Listening, 3B, 3C

Three weeks later. Debbie is phoning Pat.

Debbie	Hello Pat. I've got lots of plans for our week in London together.
Pat	OK, what are we doing?
Debbie	On Monday, your first day, we're meeting my friends.
Pat	Great!
Debbie	And we're all going to the park on Tuesday for a game of football.
Pat	I love football. What a good idea!
Debbie	On Wednesday we're visiting my boyfriend. He lives near the river.
Pat	OK.
Debbie	And on Thursday we're going to the big shops. So bring lots of money.
Pat	Ha, ha!
Debbie	Let's go to the disco on Friday evening – and stay in bed late on Saturday.
Pat	I like your plans. See you next week!

Unit 7 Listening, Let's have a party! 3A

The people are talking about special days in their countries.

1. St Patrick's Day is a very big day in Ireland. It's on March 17th. There are parades and parties in the big towns. People wear green clothes on St. Patrick's Day and they don't work.
2. In the USA we celebrate Thanksgiving in November. All the family comes together and we have lots to eat. It's very American.
3. At Halloween children in the USA dress up as witches and ghosts. Halloween is on October 31$^{st.}$ The children go to people's houses and say "Trick or treat!" People usually give them sweets.
4. I love Bonfire Night in England! On the 5th November every year we make a big fire outside. We have a party with fireworks and a barbecue.

Unit 7 Listening, 3D

All these people are talking about English-speaking countries. Listen.

a) My friend Julie and her family went to Australia. They have kangaroos, crocodiles and koalas. And Julie loves surfing there!

b) We're part of Britain, but we aren't England. I live in Scotland. You all know the Loch Ness Monster – well it comes from here. – Help!

c) We live in England but my grandparents live in Canada. Canada is near the USA and it has very cold winters. Lots of people live in cities like Montreal, Toronto or Vancouver.

d) My sister Amy lives in New Zealand now. The country has two parts. She says there are not many people in New Zealand but there are lots of sheep!

Abbildungsverzeichnis

Titel: Avenue Images GmbH (Photo Disc), Hamburg • Seite 5: iStockphoto, Calgary, Alberta; Avenue Images GmbH (Image Source RF), Hamburg; MTV Networks Europe, München; JupiterImages (RF / photos.com), Tucson, AZ • Seite 6: Avenue Images GmbH (Rubberball RF), Hamburg; Bananastock RF, Watlington / Oxon; Avenue Images GmbH (Image Source RF), Hamburg; Fotosearch RF (PhotoDisc), Waukesha, WI; Bananastock RF, Watlington / Oxon; JupiterImages (RF / photos.com), Tucson, AZ; Das Fotoarchiv, Essen • Seite 7: iStockphoto (RF / Russ), Calgary, Alberta; iStockphoto (RF / Horrocks), Calgary, Alberta; Avenue Images GmbH (Image Source RF), Hamburg; Bananastock RF, Watlington / Oxon • Seite 8: Volker Wendland, Heimsheim; Corbis (Olivier Prevosto / Photo & Co.), Düsseldorf • Seite 10: iStockphoto (RF / Weichert), Calgary, Alberta • Seite 11: JupiterImages (RF / photos.com), Tucson, AZ; Avenue Images GmbH (Corbis RF), Hamburg; Avenue Images GmbH (RF / ITStockFree), Hamburg; Avenue Images GmbH (RF / Banana), Hamburg; Getty Images RF (Photodisc / Manchan), München; Avenue Images GmbH (Digital Vision), Hamburg; • Avenue Images GmbH (Banana Stock), Hamburg; PixelQuelle.de, München • Seite 12: Avenue Images GmbH (Corbis RF), Hamburg; Alamy Images RF (RF), Abingdon, Oxon; iStockphoto (RF / Maehl), Calgary, Alberta; Fotosearch RF (Brand X Pictures), Waukesha, WI • Seite 14: iStockphoto (RF / Jamie Duplass), Calgary, Alberta • Seite 15: Picture-Alliance (Matzke), Frankfurt • Seite 17: Bananastock RF, Watlington / Oxon; JupiterImages (RF / photos.com), Tucson, AZ; Avenue Images GmbH (RF / purestock), Hamburg • Seite 18: Avenue Images GmbH (Banana Stock), Hamburg; Fotosearch RF (Brand X Pictures), Waukesha, WI; Bananastock RF, Watlington / Oxon; Bananastock RF, Watlington / Oxon • Seite 20: Dinodia, Mumbai • Seite 21: Avenue Images GmbH (Digital Vision), Hamburg • Seite 23: MEV, Augsburg; Getty Images RF (PhotoDisc), München; iStockphoto (RF / Mikula), Calgary, Alberta; Fotofinder (Caro / Teschner), Berlin; Alamy Images RM (Amengual), Abingdon, Oxon; Alamy Images RM (Enigma), Abingdon, Oxon • Seite 24: JupiterImages (RF / photos.com), Tucson, AZ; iStockphoto (RF / Jason Stitt), Calgary, Alberta; iStockphoto (RF / Katie Neudert), Calgary, Alberta; JupiterImages • Seite 26: Avenue Images GmbH (RF / Design Pics), Hamburg • Seite 27: Avenue Images GmbH (Corbis RF), Hamburg • Seite 29: Alamy Images RF (RF), Abingdon, Oxon; Getty Images (PhotoDisc), München; Avenue Images GmbH (RF / Banana), Hamburg; Fotosearch RF (Brand X Pictures), Waukesha, WI; MEV (RF), Augsburg • Seite 30: Avenue Images GmbH (Corbis RF), Hamburg • Seite 31: iStockphoto (RF / Orr), Calgary, Alberta; Andreas Staiger, Stuttgart • Seite 32: Universal Music, Hamburg; Universal Music, Hamburg • Seite 36: Avenue Images GmbH (CorbisRF), Hamburg; Fotosearch RF (PhotoDisc), Waukesha, WI; Avenue Images GmbH (Image Source), Hamburg; Inmagine (Brand X Pictures), Houston TX; iStockphoto (RF), Calgary, Alberta; Bananastock RF, Watlington / Oxon; iStockphoto (RF / Abejon), Calgary, Alberta • Seite 37: iStockphoto (RF / Watkins), Calgary, Alberta; JupiterImages (RF / photos.com), Tucson, AZ; NewsCast (Sainsbury), London; iStockphoto (RF / Madsen), Calgary, Alberta; Alamy Images RM (Helene Rogers), Abingdon, Oxon; Corel Corporation, Unterschleissheim • Seite 38: Alamy Images RM (Bubbles), Abingdon, Oxon; Alamy Images RM (J. Wiedel), Abingdon, Oxon • Seite 39: Alamy Images RM (Solloway), Abingdon, Oxon • Seite 41: iStockphoto (RF / Horne), Calgary, Alberta; iStockphoto (RF / Fairbrother), Calgary, Alberta; iStockphoto (RF / Echeverria), Calgary, Alberta; iStockphoto (RF / Spyropoulos), Calgary, Alberta; iStockphoto (RF / Hughes), Calgary, Alberta; iStockphoto (RF / Stephen Walls), Calgary, Alberta • Seite 43: Corel Corporation, Unterschleissheim; Alamy Images RM (Mica), Abingdon, Oxon; iStockphoto (RF / Craven), Calgary, Alberta; Corbis (SHANNON STAPLETON / Reuters), Düsseldorf; Getty Images RF (Photodisc), München; Visum, Hamburg; Getty Images (Image Bank / Yellow), München; MEV, Augsburg • Seite 44: Alamy Images RM (J. Wiedel), Abingdon, Oxon; Comstock, Luxemburg; Avenue Images GmbH (Corbis RF), Hamburg • Seite 45: MEV, Augsburg